Community Justice Centres

This book examines the phenomenon of Community Justice Centres and their potential to transform the justice landscape by tackling the underlying causes of crime.

Marred by recidivism, addiction, family violence, overflowing courtrooms, crippling prison spending and extreme rates of incarceration, the criminal justice system is in crisis. Community Justice Centres seek to combat this by tackling the underlying causes of crime in a particular neighbourhood and working with local people to redesign the experience of justice and enhance the notion of community. A Community Justice Centre houses a court which works with an interdisciplinary team to address the causes of criminality such as drug addiction, cognitive impairment, mental illness, poverty, abuse and intergenerational trauma. The community thus becomes a key agent of change, partnering with the Centre to tackle local issues and improve safety and community cohesion. This book, based on research into this innovative justice model, examines case studies from around the world, the challenges presented by the model and the potential for bringing its learnings into the mainstream.

This book will appeal to academics in law and criminology as well as psychology; it will also be of considerable interest to people working in the criminal justice system, including the police, government policy advisers, psychologists and social workers.

Dr Sarah Murray is a Professor of Law at the University of Western Australia Law School where she researches in the areas of constitutional law and court innovation.

Part of the
New Trajectories in Law
series
series editors
Adam Gearey
Birkbeck College, University of London

Colin Perrin
Commissioning Editor, Routledge

for information about the series and details of previous and forthcoming titles, see www.routledge.com/New-Trajectories-in-Law/book-series/NTL

A GlassHouse Book

Community Justice Centres
New Trajectories in Law

Sarah Murray

Routledge
Taylor & Francis Group
a GlassHouse Book

First published 2022
by Routledge
2 Park Square, Milton Park, Abingdon, Oxon OX14 4RN

and by Routledge
605 Third Avenue, New York, NY 10158

A GlassHouse Book

Routledge is an imprint of the Taylor & Francis Group, an informa business

© 2022 Sarah Murray

British Library Cataloguing-in-Publication Data
A catalogue record for this book is available from the British Library

Library of Congress Cataloging-in-Publication Data
A catalog record has been requested for this book

ISBN: 9780367420727 (hbk)
ISBN: 9781032137209 (pbk)
ISBN: 9780367823320 (ebk)

DOI: 10.4324/9780367823320

Typeset in Times New Roman
by Apex CoVantage, LLC

To Timothy and Jenny Ford – for being the bravest of the brave.

Contents

Preface

On my first visit to a Community Justice Centre a security guard offered me a hot chocolate and then promptly appeared with a jar of marshmallows. My PhD supervisor with his ever good humour and light-heartedness later asked me, when I recounted this unusual court experience, whether I thought the model was 'soft on justice?' Although said in jest, Community Justice Centres have often attracted these sorts of questions. This book brings together research and experiences to be able to better respond to those questions.

Community Justice Centres provide a fascinating glimpse into what bringing justice to the local level can look like. They prompt us to question the 'business as usual' operation of our legal institutions by seeking to tackle the complex web of issues that can bring someone before a court. They move beyond responding to a criminal charge to preventing them from recurring. By getting to know and connecting with the heartbeat of a neighbourhood they fashion partnerships and networks that can address both community well-being and the unique justice profile of a locale. The Community Justice Model provides an open model that each jurisdiction can make its own to begin to reconfigure the place of courts in society. In this book, I have tried to better understand what form(s) this refashioned role can take, but also what it might mean for the justice system more broadly.

Thank you to all my family and friends for your support. To Ian, Kit and Charlotte – thank you for walking with me on this community justice journey and for following me internationally to pursue it (with my daughter asking repeatedly whether we could find a Community Justice Centre where bagpipes were played!). To Deanne, Teresa, Yasmin, Laura and Miri and a host of other wonderful buddies who have helped me to keep the dream of this work alive. And to Suzie – I couldn't have got this far without you!

To my colleagues at the Law School at the University of Western Australia, you are unfailing in your support, with particular thanks to Prof. Natalie Skead, Prof. Harry Blagg, Prof. Robyn Carroll, Prof. Erika Techera and Dr Tamara Tulich, Rebecca Faugno, Dr Murray Wesson, Dr Joe Clare, Liam Elphick and Jacinta Dharmananda. I am also indebted to the UWA Fay Gale Fellowship, the UWA Institute of Advanced Studies and UWA Law Reform Research fund for assistance with much of my early Community Justice Centre research. I also thank Ava Hill-De Monchaux, Fiona Lester, Liz Richardson, Shayla Strapps, Margaret Glass, Sophie Stewart and the crew at Social Reinvestment WA for their ongoing support and interest.

I would also like to extend my gratitude to all the current and former staff of the Neighbourhood Justice Centre including Magistrate David Fanning, Louise Bassett, Jay Jordens, Hieng Lim, Ann Strunks, Rohini Thomas, Cameron Wallace, Alycia Ashcroft, Rebecca Hicks, Frederika Densley, Alison McAuliffe, Rachel Powning and many others.

I am grateful to all the members of the Therapeutic Jurisprudence Oceania Chapter as well as to the support and mentorship of Magistrate Pauline Spencer, Prof. David Wexler, Prof. Arie Freiberg, Prof. Lorana Bartels, Assoc. Prof. Becky Batagol and Rob Hulls AM.

I am thankful to those who assisted me when I visited the Centre for Court Innovation in New York City in 2018 and particularly to Adam Mansky, Mara Chin Loy, Jordan Otis, Julius Lang, Natalie Reyes, Sherene Crawford, Lauren Marker, Chris Quiones, Awinna Martinez, Yaya Yuan, Rachel Swaner, Michael Rempel, Jenn Petersen, Laura Pelcher, Jon Monsalve, Amanda Levering, Mindy Lupo and James Brodick. Thanks also to all the staff at the Red Hook Community Justice Center and to the Hon. Alex Calabrese, Amanda Berman and Viviana Gordon.

I also want to acknowledge the anonymous reviewers and the support of a large international network working and interested in Community Justice Centres including, Glenn Took, Dayna Arron, Andrea Lorenzon, Jessica Wolfe, Christine Renaud and Cateline Autixier.

1 Introduction

Court reform and the community justice centre experience – Midtown and beyond

Introduction

Like throwing a drowning man a floatation device.[1]

(Downtown Community Court, Vancouver participant)

The principle goal of a Community Justice Centre is quite simple: addressing the root causes of criminality at the grassroots level. The Community Justice Centre model focuses on reducing recidivism and social dislocation by partnering with the local community and co-locating a range of support services with a courthouse. While the model operates in varying forms, it centres on a solution-focused approach, which uses the opportunity of a court appearance as a chance to work with the defendant to address any issues that might be contributing to their offending behaviour. The first community justice pilot emerged in the Midtown area of New York City in 1993 in the Times Square precinct[2] and was followed by others in Portland, Oregon, and Red Hook, Brooklyn. There are now close to 40 in operation across the United States[3] as well as many examples worldwide, including in Canada, Australia, Israel and Scotland.[4]

This book takes on the challenge of exploring the Community Justice model and the extent to which it has the potential to change the way we interact with, and experience, justice. In looking at different examples of Community Justice Centres it investigates the opportunities and limitations of the approach exemplified by these Centres and the degree to which aspects of their operation can influence mainstream justice environments and the role/s that they undertake. It concludes by exploring the future prospects of the Community Justice model and its likely imprint on the criminal justice landscape.

DOI: 10.4324/9780367823320-1

The community justice concept and solution-focused justice

'Community justice' can mean different things in different contexts,[5] but it is often used to refer to engaging and partnering with community in undertaking a justice activity,[6] whether that be community policing, community sentencing or Community Justice Centres:

> Building upon the broken windows theory, the community policing model seeks to take police officers out of their patrol cars and integrate them into the fabric of the community, where they can better exercise both formal and informal control over conditions of disorder.° . . . In a similar fashion, the community court model aims to relocate the production of justice out of large centralized courts and into the local community.[7]

The Community Justice Centre model as a justice solution fits within a wider solution-focused movement. This, with an array of related appellations – non-adversarial justice, therapeutic jurisprudence or problem-oriented/problem-solving justice – includes a suite of court innovations, including drug courts,[8] mental health courts[9] and family violence courts.[10]

The solution-focused movement aims to recalibrate the way the justice system is conceived. Rather than as a 'system' which must continue to process defendants day-in and day-out, the movement asks whether the system can stem the tide by tackling the problems that entrap people within a cycle of offending. Solution-focused justice sees 'the authority of the courts' being harnessed 'to address the underlying problems of individual litigants, the structural problems of the justice system and the social problems of communities [through] a collaborative multidisciplinary approach'.[11] The terms 'problem-solving courts' or 'problem-solving justice' are also sometimes used; however, Freiberg has pointed to the limitations of a name which suggests that there might be only one 'problem' in an individual's life[12] and prefers the term 'problem-oriented' justice, which is 'slightly less hubristic [and] signifies the effort rather than the result'.[13] Solution-focused has the benefit of shifting away from there being a 'problem', to concentrating on what the process is directed at: finding a way or ways through a justice challenge. It has various theoretical underpinnings, which while overlapping, also diverge in their focus.

Therapeutic jurisprudence emerged in the early 1990s out of the mental health law scholarship of David Wexler and Bruce Winick.[14] Its prime contribution is to better explain how interactions with the legal system can benefit individual well-being, to the extent that legal processes allow.[15] For therapeutic jurisprudence '[t]he underlying concern is how legal systems actually function and affect people'.[16] It is interdisciplinary in focus and recommends procedural justice practices which prioritise courts treating defendants with respect and dignity and so that they feel truly heard throughout the court process.[17]

'Non-adversarial justice' has been described as 'capturing the constellation of philosophical and practical innovations currently emerging that are changing the face of the justice system' and which prioritise 'prevention', 'cooperation' and 'problem solving'.[18] It is therefore an umbrella term which can encompass other streams such as therapeutic jurisprudence and restorative justice.

Restorative justice concentrates on the 'restoration' of relationships between the victim and the offender but also the wider community.[19] This can happen parallel to court processes or independently of them, whether through sentencing circles, problem-solving meetings or victim-offender mediation.

Community Justice Centres, while drawing on aspects of all of these innovations, are distinct in housing the court inside a Centre designed and 'owned' by the local community. Unlike drug courts, family violence or mental health courts, Community Justice Centres are not focused on a singular 'problem' but rather work to address the causes and effects of local crime and distress. This 'physical presence' in the suburbs 'signals that the relationships of citizens and communities to courts differ in meaning, tone, and content'.[20] Like other solution-focused models, Community Justice Centres co-locate a range of interdisciplinary support services, including counsellors, mental health personnel, housing workers, employment officers, First Nations community liaisons and family violence staff. These allow for more holistic service provision and are in the defendant's local neighbourhood, which can in turn facilitate greater engagement. Additionally, the Centre can become a place of connection and support for local residents as they can typically access Centre services without needing to have a concurrent matter before the court.

The connection to the community is also a key feature of Community Justice Centres. Local advisory boards and volunteers keep the Centre engaged with the local community, key stakeholders and neighbourhood issues. Centre staff also work with the community to identify trouble spots in the locality at an early stage and work to provide community education, outreach and activities such as sports programs, art exhibitions and forums. What is evident in the model is a fundamental rethink of the role of the community and its place in justice processes. King has noted that:

> Court-community collaboration marks a departure from previous thinking about court's functions. Previously it was thought that the courts'

ability to address community problems was limited as the causes were beyond the courts' province. The courts were institutions apart from the community, simply there to resolve conflict by determining legal disputes and enforcing sentences and remedies. But separation from the community carries the risk of a perception that courts are ignorant of community concerns.[21]

Community Justice Centres tend to adopt a one-court/one-judicial officer model. The judicial officer gets to know the local community and works to develop strong connections across the district in which the court operates. Magistrate David Fanning from the Neighbourhood Justice Centre in Victoria, Australia, explains:

> I am the single and only judicial officer for the City of Yarra, so rather than have a number of different judicial officers or magistrates in the one court, it is just myself. So that will give consistency or hopefully give consistency in regard to sentencing and the administration of justice generally.[22]

There is considerable variation internationally in relation to the kind of offences that are heard at Community Justice Centres and the sentencing options available. One of the benefits of the model is that the court's focus can be tailored to the justice need. For instance, in the United States most Community Justice Centre courts focus on minor misdemeanours such as prostitution, theft, littering, graffiti and street drinking. As one Washington-based coordinator explained, '[i]f you deal with the quality-of-life crime, it reduces the chances that more serious crimes will also fester in those neighborhoods'.[23] Other categories or matters are also addressed, for example tenancy or family matters, such as at the Red Hook Community Justice Center, where Judge Alex Calabrese notes that 'problems don't necessarily conform to the jurisdictional boundaries of our court system'.[24] Types of cases are often heard by matter lists. The Neighbourhood Justice Centre for instance has a Victorian Civil and Administrative Tribunal (VCAT) list along with Family Violence hearing days once per week for which special safety arrangements are in place. It also hosts monthly Aboriginal Hearing Days where Aboriginal and Torres Strait Islander service agencies and community members are in attendance and when Aboriginal and Torres Strait Islanders appearing before the court can elect to have their matters heard.

The emergence of community justice

Times Square in New York City – the tourist mecca and heart of Broadway – was ravaged by petty crime, prostitution and drug offending across the 1970s and 1980s.[25] Described by Mayor Michael Bloomberg 'as the quality-of-life crime capital of the city',[26] the justice system was struggling to cope. The New York court system had moved to a more centralised model which sentenced offenders often without the detailed knowledge of their communities or circumstances.[27] Times Square's reputation as a risky place to visit became hard to shake. With the rise of 'broken window'[28] policing in the 1980s and 1990s new ways of tackling crime began to emerge, including the Midtown Community Court.

After much development and the establishment of a network of partnerships across the local area, the Midtown Community Court opened its doors in 1993. As Greg Berman describes:

> Located on a busy side street not far from Times Square, the Midtown Community Court occupies a 100-year-old building that was formerly a magistrate courthouse. The planning team put great effort into the physical design of the courthouse, making it complement and reflect the programmatic vision of the experiment. For example, the holding area for defendants featured clean, well-lit areas secured with specially-treated glass panels – a marked contrast to the squalid holding pens with iron bars in many urban courthouses. A full floor of office space was devoted to an on-site clinic staffed by social workers and alternative sanction staff responsible for working directly with defendants. And the building was wired for an innovative computer system that allowed the judge, attorneys, and social service providers to keep in touch with each other and access information about defendants at the click of a mouse.[29]

Its mission was to connect better with defendants but also with the local community. The court used the legal moment to provide offenders with support services to help get their lives back on track. However, it also allowed the community to begin to believe that change was possible by putting offenders to work locally in removing graffiti tagging and collecting rubbish. As Sviridoff et al. recognise, it was about conceiving of 'communities as victims too'.[30] Early evaluations over the next few years were positive and other communities were watching.

By 4 March 1998, after a visit to Midtown Community Court by the local district attorney,[31] Portland, Oregon, followed suit with a Community Court pilot in Multnomah County declaring that:

> The Community Court Project endeavors to address quality-of-life crime that diminishes citizens' pride and sense of safety in their neighborhoods. By collaborating with citizens, law enforcement, court and social service agencies, the Community Court Project encourages

defendants to contribute positively to their community through community service projects and offers them social service assistance to address underlying problems that can lead to criminal behavior.[32]

Its inaugural Judge was said to have made offenders write repeat lines, '*I will not steal from Safeway*', like students in detention.[33] For most defendants a plea of guilty will result in an order to undertake community work or engage with relevant services.[34]

Hartford Community Court then followed, serving five towns alongside Hartford.[35] Two years later the Red Hook Community Justice Center in Brooklyn, New York, opened in a refurbished schoolhouse on Visitation Place after broad community consultation and with the ongoing work of the Center for Court Innovation. The Red Hook Center has been one of the most innovative Community Justice exemplars, exploring Navajo-influenced peacemaking initiatives, a Public Safety Corps and intensive community partnerships and engagement.[36]

As new Community Justice sites continued to emerge in the United States so did examples worldwide, including the United Kingdom, Australia and Canada. The North Liverpool Community Justice Centre commenced in 2005[37] (although closing some eight years later) and the first Australian archetype, the Neighbourhood Justice Centre, was opened in the City of Yarra, Victoria, in 2007. As they have burgeoned, so have their inventiveness. Since 2013, the Spokane Municipal Community Court in Washington has operated on a weekly basis out of a public library.[38] The Brownsville Community Justice Center was originally planned to operate alongside a new court complex but continued as a standalone Center, even when court approvals by the City of New York were abandoned.[39]

Community court – challenges and opportunities?

Chapter 2 traces the core features of the Community Justice Model. Chapter 3 sets out a number of case studies to provide a more granular understanding of how Centres can operate, what attributes they share and what bespoke aspects emerge from one community to another.

A pivotal issue that has emerged in the Community Justice context is how Centres can track failures and success and find ways to do so consistently. Even if Community Justice Centres adequately track and report on their performance, there is a need to consistently prove their value for money. Chapter 4 will address some of these issues and will look particularly at the experience of the North Liverpool Community Justice Centre. This Centre was closed by the government after eight years of operation for a range of reasons, but the data collected proved a key obstacle to the Centre continuing.[40] Chapter 4 will also address criticisms of the Community Justice model, including questions surrounding the change in the role of the court and the judicial officer. Is the legal entry point the best way to trace the source of social 'problems'[41] and address community disadvantage? Can a court and court-annexed services addressing underlying issues bring about other procedural and paternalistic concerns? If defendants accept support to address addictions or mental health conditions at the court door does that compromise individual agency? Is this combining justice with treatment and what implications does that bring?[42] It is questions such as these which will be further explored in Chapter 4.

Chapter 5 looks at one of the real challenges for the model which has been the degree to which its learning can be mainstreamed or whether it can only be operationalised as a standalone justice centre. Certainly, restorative justice and therapeutic tools are found in other solution-focused courts (as well as specialised lists) such as drug courts or mental health courts. However, unlike Community Justice Centres, these courts are more focused on addressing a targeted justice 'problem' than working with a particular neighbourhood or local community. One of the key benefits to mainstreaming is ensuring equity of access to the justice model for citizens. Mainstreaming, however, presents a host of related questions: to what extent is the widespread resourcing of agencies and linked supports feasible? How can centralised courts retain the community connection of standard Community Justice Centres? What is needed to roll out Community Justice principles on a wider scale and to bring about the necessary cultural change and training that courts and court personnel require? If mainstreaming is possible what are the implications of it for the justice system as a whole?

Chapter 6 brings the book to a conclusion by looking ahead to the likely future of the Community Justice innovation and what prospects and challenges it is liable to face.

Conclusion

For the justice space, learning about what works and what does not is vital to improve community outcomes and stem rising prison costs and justice budgets. Better understanding the Community Justice Centres movement allows us to see what potential and risk may lie in bringing our justice responses to the local level. What are the implications of providing social services through justice avenues? What does Community Justice mean for individual agency? How does a Justice Centre find and work with a 'community' and what dangers can this present? Are there any implications for judicial ethics? What represents best practice in the Community Justice space? How might such innovations change community perceptions and expectations of courts and justice agencies? If Community Justice Centres can radically improve a community's justice profile and cohesion, does that upset what can be delivered by more mainstream courts, or can these become pilots for broader justice reforms? There is also a need to ask whether, if lessons can be learnt, to what extent are these unique to particular justice environments or court cultures? Ultimately, the Community Justice Centre experiment presents a chance to ask whether it can be cast as a justice movement and, if so, what this might augur for how we define the boundaries of justice systems and what such systems can achieve for the communities they serve.

Notes

1 Margaret Jackson, William Glackman and Christopher Giles, 'Downtown Community Court Participant Survey II', 2012, 155, https://www2.gov.bc.ca/assets/gov/law-crime-and-justice/courthouse-services/community-court/dcc-research-compilation.pdf
2 Sarah Murray, 'Keeping It in the Neighbourhood? Neighbourhood Courts in the Australian Context' (2009) 35 *Monash University Law Review* 74; Greg Berman and John Feinblatt, *Good Courts – The Case for Problem-Solving Justice* (New York Press, 2005) 61.
3 Julius Lang, *What Is a Community Court? How the Model Is Being Adapted Across the United States* (Bureau of Justice Assistance, 2011) 14, www.courtinnovation.org/sites/default/files/documents/What%20is%20a%20Community%20Court.pdf
4 Robert V. Wolf, 'Community Justice Around the Globe: An International Overview' (2006) 22 *Crime & Justice International* 4.
5 See, e.g. Greg Berman and Aubrey Fox, 'From the Margins to the Mainstream: Community Justice at the Crossroads' (2001) 22(2) *Justice System Journal* 189, 191–2.
6 See, e.g. David R. Karp and Todd R. Clear, 'Community Justice: A Conceptual Framework' (2000) 2 *Criminal Justice* 323.
7 Cynthia Lee et al., *A Community Court Grows in Brooklyn: A Comprehensive Evaluation of the Red Hook Community Justice Center – Executive Summary* (National Centre for State Courts, 2013) 2. See also Michele Sviridoff, David Rottman, Brian Ostrom and Richard Curtis, *Dispensing Justice Locally – The Implementation and Effects of the Midtown Community Court* (Harwood Academic Publishers, 2000) 7–8.
8 James L. Nolan, *Reinventing Justice – The American Drug Court Movement* (Princeton University Press, 2003).
9 Michelle Edgely, 'Why Do Mental Health Courts Work? A Confluence of Treatment, Support and Adroit Judicial Supervision' (2014) 37 *International Journal of Law & Psychiatry* 572; Lorraine Lim and Andrew Day, 'Mental Health Diversion Courts: Some Directions for Further Development' (2013) 20(1) *Psychiatry, Psychology and Law* 36.
10 Michael King and Becky Batagol, 'Enforcer, Manager or Leader? The Judicial Role in Family Violence Courts' (2010) 33 *International Journal of Law and Psychiatry* 406.
11 Greg Berman and John Feinblatt, 'Judges and Problem-Solving Courts', 2002, www.courtinnovation.org/sites/default/files/JudgesProblemSolvingCourts1.pdf

12 Arie Freiberg, 'Problem-Oriented Courts: Innovative Solutions to Intractable Problems?' (2011) 11 *Journal of Judicial Administration* 8, 22.
13 Ibid. 25, endnote 5.
14 See, e.g., David Wexler, *Therapeutic Jurisprudence – The Law as a Therapeutic Agent* (Carolina Academic Press, 1990); David Wexler and Bruce Winick (eds), *Essays in Therapeutic Jurisprudence* (Carolina Academic Press, 1991); David Wexler and Bruce Winick (eds), *Law in a Therapeutic Key: Developments in Therapeutic Jurisprudence* (Carolina Academic Press, 1996).
15 See, Bruce Arrigo, 'The Ethics of Therapeutic Jurisprudence: A Critical and Theoretical Enquiry of Law, Psychology and Crime' (2004) 11 *Psychiatry, Psychology and Law* 23; Michael King, 'Restorative Justice, Therapeutic Jurisprudence and the Rise of Emotionally Intelligent Justice' (2008) 32(3) *Melbourne University Law Review* 1096; Michael L. Perlin, 'Have You Seen Dignity? The Story of the Development of Therapeutic Jurisprudence' (2007) 27 *New Zealand Universities Law Review* 1135.
16 David Wexler, 'Two Decades of Therapeutic Jurisprudence' (2008) 24 *Touro Law Review* 17, 20.
17 Tom Tyler, *Why People Obey the Law* (Princeton University Press, 1990); John Thibaut and Laurens Walker, *Procedural Justice: A Psychological Analysis* (Lawrence Erlbaum Associates, 1975).
18 Michael King, Arie Freiberg, Becky Batagol and Ross Hyams, *Non-Adversarial Justice* (Federation Press, 2009) 5.
19 John Braithwaite, 'Restorative Justice and a Better Future' in Eugene McLaughlin, Ross Fergusson, Gordon Hughes and Louise Westmarland (eds), *Restorative Justice- Critical Issues* (Sage Publications, 2003) 56–7; Heather Strang and John Braithwaite (eds), *Restorative Justice and Civil Society* (Cambridge University Press, 2001).
20 Jeffrey Fagan and Victoria Malkin, 'Theorizing Community Justice Through Community Courts' (2003) XXX *Fordham Urban Law Journal* 897, 898.
21 Michael King, 'What Can Mainstream Courts Learn from Problem-Solving Courts' (2007) 32(2) *Alternative Law Journal* 91, 94.
22 Anita Barraud, 'One-Stop Legal Shop', *The Law Report – ABC Radio National*, 3 April 2007, www.abc.net.au/radionational/programs/lawreport/one-stop-legal-shop/3400580
23 Sarah Schweig, *Beyond a Single Neighborhood* (Centre for Court Innovation, 2014) 2.
24 Center for Court Innovation, 'Alex Calabrese, Judge, Red Hook Community Justice Center – Interview' , 2005, https://www.courtinnovation.org/publications/alex-calabrese-judge-red-hook-community-justice-center
25 Greg Berman, *Principles of Community Justice – A Guide for Community Court Planners* (Center for Court Innovation, 2010) 3.
26 Greg Berman, 'Problem-Solving Justice in New York: Reflections on 15 Years of Judicial Reform' (2008) 10(2) *Government Law & Policy Journal* 30.
27 Ibid.
28 Which developed out of the early paper by James Q. Wilson and George L. Kelling, 'Broken Windows – The Police and Neighborhood Safety' (1982) March *The Atlantic Monthly* www.theatlantic.com/magazine/archive/1982/03/broken-windows/304465/; see Kelling's discussion of the innovation in 'How New York Became Safe: The Full Story' (2009) *City Journal*, www.city-journal.org/html/how-new-york-became-safe-full-story-13197.html; Berman and Feinblatt, *Good Courts*, above n 2, 48–9 refer to 'problem-solving courts stand[ing]

on the shoulders of broken-windows and problem-oriented policing'. While Chief Judge Kaye has explained the rise of the community court movement as a response to the widened policing net: Judith S. Kaye, 'Delivering Justice Today: A Problem-Solving Approach' (2004) 22 *Yale Law & Policy Review* 125, 130–1.

29 Berman, *Principles of Community Justice*, above n 25, 3.

30 Michele Sviridoff, David Rottman, Brian Ostrom and Richard Curtis, *Dispensing Justice Locally – The Implementation and Effects of the Midtown Community Court* (Harwood Academic Publishers, 2000) 7.

31 Berman and Feinblatt, *Good Courts*, above n 2, 71.

32 Ibid. 67.

33 Aimee Green, 'A Sentence With a Second Chance', *The Oregonian*, 23 October 2008, www.oregonlive.com/portland/2008/10/a_sentence_with_a_second_chanc.html

34 See, e.g. Multnomah County District Attorney, 'Community Court', www.mcda.us/index.php/community-initiatives-special-programs/community-court/

35 Center for Court Innovation, 'Mentor Community Courts', www.courtinnovation.org/mentor-community-courts

36 Center for Court Innovation, 'Fact Sheet: Peacemaking Programs', www.courtinnovation.org/publications/fact-sheet-peacemaking-programs; see further chapter 3.

37 The Centre closed in 2013 as discussed further in chapter 4.

38 Spokane Public Library, 'Community Court', www.spokanelibrary.org/community-court/

39 Greg Berman, *Advancing Community Justice: The Challenge of Brownsville, Brooklyn* (Center for Court Innovation, 2013) 9, www.courtinnovation.org/publications/advancing-community-justice-challenge-brownsville-brooklyn

40 See chapter 4 and Sarah Murray and Harry Blagg, 'Reconceptualising Community Justice Centre Evaluations – Lessons from the North Liverpool Experience' (2018) 27(2) *Griffith Law Review* 254.

41 Freiberg, above n 12, 21–2.

42 Harry Blagg, ' "A Problem Shared. . . ?" Some Reflections on Problem Solving Courts and Court Innovation in Australia' (2013) 1 *Plymouth Law and Criminal justice Review* 24, 26.

Bibliography

Arrigo, Bruce. 'The Ethics of Therapeutic Jurisprudence: A Critical and Theoretical Enquiry of Law, Psychology and Crime' (2004) 11 *Psychiatry, Psychology and Law* 23.

Barraud, Anita. 'One-Stop Legal Shop' *The Law Report – ABC Radio National*, 3 April 2007, www.abc.net.au/radionational/programs/lawreport/one-stop-legal-shop/3400580

Berman, Greg. *Advancing Community Justice: The Challenge of Brownsville, Brooklyn* (Center for Court Innovation, 2013), www.courtinnovation.org/publications/advancing-community-justice-challenge-brownsville-brooklyn

Berman, Greg. *Principles of Community Justice – A Guide for Community Court Planners* (Center for Court Innovation, 2010).

Berman, Greg. 'Problem-Solving Justice in New York: Reflections on 15 Years of Judicial Reform' (2008) 10(2) *Government Law & Policy Journal* 30.

Berman, Greg and John Feinblatt. *Good Courts – The Case for Problem-Solving Justice* (New York Press, 2005).

Berman, Greg and John Feinblatt. 'Judges and Problem-Solving Courts', 2002, www.courtinnovation.org/sites/default/files/JudgesProblemSolvingCourts1.pdf

Berman, Greg and Aubrey Fox. 'From the Margins to the Mainstream: Community Justice at the Crossroads' (2001) 22(2) *Justice System Journal* 189.

Blagg, Harry. '"A Problem Shared. . . ?" Some Reflections on Problem Solving Courts and Court Innovation in Australia' (2013) 1 *Plymouth Law and Criminal Justice Review* 24.

Center for Court Innovation. 'Alex Calabrese, Judge, Red Hook Community Justice Center – Interview' , 2005, https://www.courtinnovation.org/publications/alex-calabrese-judge-red-hook-community-justice-center

Center for Court Innovation. 'Fact Sheet: Peacemaking Programs', www.courtinnovation.org/publications/fact-sheet-peacemaking-programs

Center for Court Innovation. 'Mentor Community Courts', www.courtinnovation.org/mentor-community-courts

Edgely, Michelle. 'Why Do Mental Health Courts Work? A Confluence of Treatment, Support and Adroit Judicial Supervision' (2014) 37 *International Journal of Law & Psychiatry* 572.

Fagan, Jeffrey and Victoria Malkin. 'Theorizing Community Justice Through Community Courts' (2003) XXX *Fordham Urban Law Journal* 897.

Freiberg, Arie. 'Problem-Oriented Courts: Innovative Solutions to Intractable Problems?' (2011) 11 *Journal of Judicial Administration* 8.

Green, Aimee. 'A Sentence with a Second Chance', *The Oregonian*, 23 October 2008, www.oregonlive.com/portland/2008/10/a_sentence_with_a_second_chanc.html

Jackson, Margaret, William Glackman and Christopher Giles. 'Downtown Community Court Participant Survey II', 2012, https://www2.gov.bc.ca/assets/gov/law-crime-and-justice/courthouse-services/community-court/dcc-research-compilation.pdf

Karp, David R. and Todd R. Clear. 'Community Justice: A Conceptual Framework' (2000) 2 *Criminal Justice* 323.

Kaye, Judith S. 'Delivering Justice Today: A Problem-Solving Approach' (2004) 22 *Yale Law & Policy Review* 125.

Kelling, George L. 'How New York Became Safe: The Full Story' (2009) *City Journal*, www.city-journal.org/html/how-new-york-became-safe-full-story-13197.html

King, Michael. 'Restorative Justice, Therapeutic Jurisprudence and the Rise of Emotionally Intelligent Justice' (2008) 32(3) *Melbourne University Law Review* 1096.

King, Michael. 'What Can Mainstream Courts Learn from Problem-Solving Courts' (2007) 32(2) *Alternative Law Journal* 91.

King, Michael and Becky Batagol. 'Enforcer, Manager or Leader? The Judicial Role in Family Violence Courts' (2010) 33 *International Journal of Law and Psychiatry* 406.

King, Michael, Arie Freiberg, Becky Batagol and Ross Hyams. *Non-Adversarial Justice* (Federation Press, 2009, 2nd edn 2014).

Lang, Julius. *What Is a Community Court? How the Model Is Being Adapted Across the United States* (Bureau of Justice Assistance, 2011), www.courtinnovation.org/sites/default/files/documents/What%20is%20a%20Community%20Court.pdf

Lee, Cynthia G. et al. *A Community Court Grows in Brooklyn: A Comprehensive Evaluation of the Red Hook Community Justice Center – Executive Summary* (National Centre for State Courts, 2013).

Lim, Lorraine and Andrew Day. 'Mental Health Diversion Courts: Some Directions for Further Development' (2013) 20(1) *Psychiatry, Psychology and Law* 36.

McLaughlin, Eugene, Ross Fergusson, Gordon Hughes and Louise Westmarland (eds). *Restorative Justice- Critical Issues* (Sage Publications, 2003).

Multnomah County District Attorney. 'Community Court', www.mcda.us/index.php/community-initiatives-special-programs/community-court/

Murray, Sarah. 'Keeping It in the Neighbourhood? Neighbourhood Courts in the Australian Context' (2009) 35 *Monash University Law Review* 74.

Murray, Sarah and Harry Blagg. 'Reconceptualising Community Justice Centre Evaluations – Lessons from the North Liverpool Experience' (2018) 27(2) *Griffith Law Review* 254.

Nolan, James L. *Reinventing Justice – The American Drug Court Movement* (Princeton University Press, 2003).

Perlin, Michael L. 'Have You Seen Dignity? The Story of the Development of Therapeutic Jurisprudence' (2007) 27 *New Zealand Universities Law Review* 1135.

Schweig, Sarah. *Beyond a Single Neighborhood* (Centre for Court Innovation, 2014).

Spokane Public Library. 'Community Court', www.spokanelibrary.org/community-court/

Strang, Heather and John Braithwaite (eds). *Restorative Justice and Civil Society* (Cambridge University Press, 2001).

Sviridoff, Michelle, David Rottman, Brian Ostrom and Richard Curtis. *Dispensing Justice Locally – The Implementation and Effects of the Midtown Community Court* (Harwood Academic Publishers, 2000).

Thibaut, John and Laurens Walker. *Procedural Justice: A Psychological Analysis* (Lawrence Erlbaum Associates, 1975).

Tyler, Tom. *Why People Obey the Law* (Princeton University Press, 1990).

Wexler, David. *Therapeutic Jurisprudence – The Law as a Therapeutic Agent* (Carolina Academic Press, 1990).

Wexler, David. 'Two Decades of Therapeutic Jurisprudence' (2008) 24 *Touro Law Review* 17.

Wexler, David and Bruce Winick (eds). *Essays in Therapeutic Jurisprudence* (Carolina Academic Press, 1991).

Wexler, David and Bruce Winick (eds). *Law in a Therapeutic Key: Developments in Therapeutic Jurisprudence* (Carolina Academic Press, 1996).

Wilson, James Q. and George L. Kelling. 'Broken Windows – The Police and Neighborhood Safety' (1982) March *The Atlantic Monthly*, www.theatlantic.com/magazine/archive/1982/03/broken-windows/304465/

Wolf, Robert V. 'Community Justice Around the Globe: An International Overview' (2006) 22 *Crime & Justice International* 4.

2 The Community Justice Centre model

Introduction

Community courts are not designed to be cookie-cutter models; in a perfect world, each will be specifically tailored to reflect the needs of the neighborhood it serves.[1]

The Community Justice Centre model, while it does vary from centre to centre, typically co-locates a court with a host of other services. The goal is for the work of the court to be done in a more holistic way. Interdisciplinary services can work with individuals coming before the court, or who are part of the local community, to help them work through life challenges such as homelessness, mental health, financial stability, employment or addiction, which often underpin ongoing engagement with the criminal justice system. The Centre also engages with the community to prevent crime, educate residents and businesses and address local concerns. As Magistrate Fanning from the Neighbourhood Justice Centre has observed:

> The narrative of the NJC [Neighbourhood Justice Centre] is sometimes difficult to get right. What is the NJC? What is community justice? On one hand it is a court, on the other hand it is a community centre. I think it can be a real challenge to explain the NJC because it is so unusual in the sense of having so many services located in the one place. And also in terms of having a community engagement focus.[2]

The co-location of a court, typically with one judicial officer, puts the bench in a unique position to shape the court process and to acquire a deep knowledge of the local community. The court draws on that knowledge and the support of the wrap-around service team to handle court matters in a more therapeutic and solution-focused way. As one Legal Aid Lawyer at

DOI: 10.4324/9780367823320-2

the Neighbourhood Justice Centre put it, the approach unpacks the challenge facing many lower-tier criminal courts: '[a]re people being sentenced because of the crime they committed (and they are), but are they also being sentenced because of the conditions they have?'[3]

Some of the key features of the model are explained in this chapter, including the collaborative and solution-focused approach, local knowledge, community engagement and crime prevention, the emphasis on process, individualising the bench, collecting data and community planning. However, it is important to remember that each Centre is unique and is self-defining while operating within the broad Community Justice theme. For example, the Brownsville Community Justice Center, as outlined in detail in Chapter 3, does not accommodate a courthouse. While the Center was originally planned to model the Red Hook Community Justice Center, the planned co-location of the court did not proceed. This has meant that the Brownsville Community Justice Center is an example of a Community Justice Centre that has extensive community engagement projects and works with offenders but without a judicial officer based at the Center. Similarly, some Centres have particular areas of focus. For example the Harlem Community Justice Center specialises in housing, juvenile justice and parole supervision while the Spokane Municipal Community Court has been operating once a week from a local library with a focus on homelessness.

Collaborative and solution-focused

> *Everything is incorporated into one. I can get all the info I need in one place.*[4]

The model provides a 'one-stop-shop'[5] approach to service provision where the court, support services and defendant can work in partnership to unravel the issues that brought that person before the court. At the Downtown Community Court in Vancouver one study found that '[r]espondents believed that the reported main strengths of DCC were that resources were contained in one site – especially health and housing'.[6] This collaboration is designed to address the consistent problem of individuals missing out on assistance or getting lost in the referral mill by having the ability to immediately make service linkages.

The model also means that the judicial officer can, depending on the court, defer sentencing and facilitate an individual to engage with wrap-around drug counselling, mental health support or housing assistance to put them in a better position to complete their community order and the conditions it imposes. This can mean that accessing the supports has the added authority or imprimatur of the court and can provide an added incentive to engage. One issue that has been raised, and which is explored further in Chapter 4, is whether the curial connection can taint the voluntariness of the service engagement. However, there is no compulsion to interact with the wrap-around service team, and some defendants may not be ready to do so. It may mean that the judicial officer can work through any obstacles with the defendant and their lawyer at their next court appearance. It also may mean that a more traditional sentencing approach is adopted. As Frazer notes:

> Changing a defendant's behavior is difficult, especially when avoiding criminal behavior requires a serious shift in lifestyle or livelihood. Community courts are premised at least in part on the belief that defendants undergoing this kind of change need a supportive structure to improve their chances of success.[7]

But it is also the case that not all matters require a solution-focused response, and in some instances offences may be dealt with in a similar way to downtown courts. What is evident is that there is an emphasis on offenders being accountable for their actions whether that be through community service in the local area, attending programs or in some cases, doing time in jail. As Judge Calabrese explains:

> A typical sentence can include mandatory drug treatment, job training, adult education classes, community service or a combination. The community benefits directly not only from the mandated community service – such as painting over graffiti and cleaning local parks – but, more importantly, by having a member of the community get to the root of his or her criminal activity and address it.[8]

Much of this depends on the type of matters dealt with by the court whether they hear more minor offences or, whether like the Neighbourhood Justice Centre or the San Francisco Community Justice Center, the court has jurisdiction to address more serious matters.

It is also the case that with many Community Justice Centres, all residents in the community are able to access the Centre's services and engage in its activities even if they do not have a court matter at the Centre.[9] As a Neighbourhood Justice Centre staff member describes, '[t]he NJC is a centre with a court within it. Not a court with a centre around it'.[10]

The approach to contested matters varies between Centres. At the Neighbourhood Justice Centre, for instance, the court is resourced to deal mainly with matters in which there is a plea of guilty, with contested matters redirected to the central law courts. One of the criticisms of such models, which is addressed further in Chapter 4, is that defendants can feel under pressure to plead guilty to obtain access to court-annexed services that are not always available in mainstream courts.[11] At the Red Hook Community Justice Center, however, contested and uncontested matters are dealt with by the Center's Judge, although some support and treatment options, such as for drug addiction, are conditional on a guilty plea.

Co-located agencies can also include other government agencies such as social security providers, lawyers, police and corrections teams. At the Neighbourhood Justice Centre these teams are all located in a large open-plan space. While this has required the development of privacy and information protocols, it has allowed for good working relationships which facilitate service provision at the Centre. While some services are funded by the Centre's budget, many local providers choose to co-locate at the Centre because of the efficiencies it brings. Other than the provision of space and relevant overheads, this often comes at no financial cost to the Centre.[12]

The key benefit of the in-house availability of service provision is the immediacy of the engagement with services. As one client at the Neighbourhood Justice Centre commented in an evaluation, 'All the services were in the same building. There was no time wasted on finding the right help'.[13] Defendants are sometimes sentenced to attend programs run out of the Centre. For example, the South Dallas Community Court runs in-house programs directed at local prostitution and truancy.[14] Similarly the Midtown Community Court runs programs such as UPNEXT which provides parenting and employment support and training.[15]

One study has found that this engagement can be strengthened because of the long-term connections that can often be established and which can then flow on to 'warm referrals' to stable assistance providers in the local area.[16] But the model's strength can also be a hindrance in some cases as investigated further in Chapter 4. Engaging with services may be perfunctory, strategic and potentially hinder lasting change in an individual's circumstances. At Vancouver's Downtown Community Court one report found that:

> respondents suggested that a real commitment on the part of offenders and the understanding of behaviors were essential, and while there may be short- term improvements, the greatest challenges would be assisting those with mental health issues and addictions to change long-term patterns of behavior.[17]

However, while defendants may be introduced to these services as part of the resolution of their matter, they can always choose to cease ongoing engagement, even if this means failing to meet some of the conditions of their order.

In-depth local knowledge

One of the significant innovations with the Community Justice Centre model is embedding courthouses at the neighbourhood level. This not only means that the court has greater knowledge of the local area but that the residents can come to see the Centre and the court as part of the community rather than separated from it.[18] There is also the potential for the Centre to involve the community in a targeted way with the Centre's activities which can also contribute to community cohesion and an increase in trust in the justice system.[19]

The local embeddedness means that Centre staff are able to have a unique grasp of the community landscape and dynamics, are well connected with residents, agencies, business owners and schools in the area and have a particular sense of their needs and challenges. This can then also flow through to the management of the court and the way the court list is managed. Many Centres have special hearings on particular days along with relevant support services. For instance, the South Dallas Community Court has a parole list[20] while the Neighbourhood Justice Centre has a Family Violence day once per week and Aboriginal Hearing days monthly.[21]

The size of the community served by a Community Justice Centre can vary considerably.[22] For instance, the Hartford Community Court works across 17 distinct suburban areas; the Seattle Community Court expanded its operation to the whole city; while the Midtown Community Court has a particular focus on Times Square and surrounds but hears prostitution offences from across Manhattan.[23] Washington DC trialled an innovative method of connecting with community across the city whereby the central metropolitan court created 'community court calendars' in which each Washington court judge was allocated to a particular police district and developed connections and local knowledge with that assigned area.[24]

Community engagement and crime prevention

The model has also tended to favour prophylactic approaches to crime prevention by working closely with the community to address tensions or emerging problems early-on rather than just taking a matter-by-matter approach.[25] As noted in relation to the operations at the Downtown Community Court in Vancouver:

> The justice system cannot solve complex social and crime problems by itself. The community court works with partners in the health and social service systems, and the community.[26]

At the Red Hook Community Justice Center for instance, Judge Calabrese recounts one example where:

> One of the local schools called us to say that a group of kids were starting to form a gang. We responded immediately. I went to the school to talk to the students. Our clinical director put together an anger management curriculum. A court officer who grew up in the neighborhood offered to talk to the kids about his perspective as a member of the community. And the Brooklyn District Attorney's Office brought in a former gang member who runs anti-violence programs around the country.[27]

Central to the model is the role of the community.[28] At the Neighbourhood Justice Centre the Program and Innovation Team works on community initiatives, community education and engages with key stakeholders to develop connections and trust such as the Collingwood Living in Harmony Project designed to reduce family violence in migrant communities, the Reporting of Crime Project in local housing estates and the Yarra Communities that Care Project to focus on the health of young people in the area.[29] The Red Hook Community Justice Center has numerous programs in which residents can get involved, including through the Center's Peacemaking, Resident Empowerment, Youth Court or 'Bridging the Gap' Programs. Similarly, the Midtown Community Court has a Community Conditions Panel including local police as well as business and community representatives who can discuss what is working well and what challenges remain for the local area.[30] One of the challenges is to ensure that a suitable cross-section of stakeholders engage with the Centre to reflect the heterogeneity and diversity of the neighbourhood/s served.[31]

Typically, the community helps to co-design and co-create the Centre, including where it is positioned. This grassroots involvement has been hailed as key to the success of the Red Hook Community Justice Center and the Neighbourhood Justice Centre, while the community's more limited involvement and buy-in to the North Liverpool Community Justice Centre was also flagged as a reason for its eventual closure.[32] Greg Berman explained that the involvement of the community early on and use of 'focus groups . . . sent a powerful message to Red Hook residents. . . . And that message was: your voice counts'.[33] Partnering with the community also allows for locals to buy in to the Centre and its activities. In the Vancouver Downtown Community Court one way this was achieved was in collaborating with partners to bring local artists to design murals in the building to 'humanize the face of justice'.[34]

The interaction of the court with the community is typically beyond what can be achieved in a mainstream court. One of the concerns that can flow from this is whether it will undermine the judicial role or compromise the independence or impartiality of the bench. This issue is discussed further in Chapter 4 along with how and whether Centres operate to counter this concern.

A focus on process

Procedural justice or ensuring that priority is given to an individual's experience of the court process is replicated across solution-focused models, including Community Justice Centres. The goal is for participants, who may feel disempowered, to feel respected as individuals and to be given agency and a space to be heard. This is facilitated by the interactions and relationships that can develop between the defendant and the judicial officer as well as with the Centre staff. It can be facilitated by steps, including making sure that a participant understands the order that is being proposed and showing an awareness of the participant's life circumstances and how they are likely to be affected by the terms of the order. Procedural justice research, including across Community Justice Centres, highlights how focusing on the dignity of participants and the care with which they are treated can contribute significantly to the perceived legitimacy of the process, trust of staff and sentence compliance.[35] Community respect for the judicial officer and procedurally fair processes can have a significant impact on the way that the court is perceived as can other aspects such as court design.[36] It is something that is frequently commented on in Centre evaluations:

I'm mostly happy because I had a chance to explain and to be able to speak openly about some things.

[Downtown Community Court][37]

. . .

Being treated politely, courteously and respectfully by all the staff at the Client Services.

[Neighbourhood Justice Centre][38]

. . .

He allows you to speak. I got a good feel from [Judge] Calabrese because of the fact that he likes to interact and get your opinion. I don't get the feeling that he's one of those judges that that [sic] looks down on people. To me, he's fair, I'll put it that way. The court officers treat you like a person too, not like that other court over there. I learned that there's two different types of ways that courts treat people. You have these obnoxious goons and then you have those that look at you like, ok, you made a mistake.

[Red Hook Community Justice Center][39]

At the Red Hook Community Justice Center, one evaluation found that given a choice of responses, defendants assessed the judge to be 'more compassionate' (48.7%), 'more fair' (27.4%) or 'more connected to people' (11.1%) (with 17.9% selecting 'no difference').[40] Judge Fletcher, who was assigned to the North Liverpool Community Justice Centre, indicated that the judicial-defendant relationship was key:

When I don't speak to their lawyer and just speak to them, you see a look of surprise. I think the vast majority have found it useful because they can tell me what's on their minds and I find it more useful than finding out what their lawyer thinks is going on.[41]

In adopting less adversarial, more collaborative models of operation, the movement has faced criticisms that the rights of the defendant and strong advocacy can begin to fall away.[42] The role of defence counsel and the place of due process is addressed in further detail in Chapter 4.

Individualising the bench

The community connection is heightened by the assignment of a single judicial officer to the court based at the Community Justice Centre. This judicial officer is able to bring a deep knowledge of the neighbourhood to the role. At the North Liverpool Community Justice Centre it was said that:

I've heard people in the pub talking and a lot of it is directed towards Mr Fletcher [often 'Fletch'] . . . not just as a Judge but as an individual, you can see how much passion he has and he wants to try and help the community and he really does understand your pitfalls and the man really does want to help.[43]

This connection can also instil greater confidence and legitimacy in the judicial monitoring role as well as having the 'judicial authority to rein force . . . progress'.[44] This faith in the judicial officer has been shown to be a particularly significant determinant of heightened perceptions of fairness in the court process.[45] Participants will often appear regularly before the court to reflect on compliance with goals that have been set and to discuss challenges that have been encountered along the way. As explained by Magistrate Pauline Spencer:

> stopping offending involves the process of the person gradually getting stronger, of engaging with services, and coming to the realisation that they need to stop the alcohol or drugs. . . . [T]he court can take them on that process and it can be very powerful to have the same judicial officer engaging with the person and motivating them, by saying, for example, 'You're doing well' or 'That is not so great. Why did it happen?'. This builds a relationship with the person over time, helping them to recover.[46]

Similarly at the Neighbourhood Justice Centre Magistrate David Fanning uses judicial monitoring in some cases to encourage a participant to take advantage of the help available:

> If there is non-compliance during the deferred sentencing period, Magistrate Fanning will express concern at what has occurred, while at the same time emphasising that it is ultimately their choice whether or not they seek to address their issues and/or to reoffend. In Magistrate Fanning's view, such an expression of disappointment is not antithetical to the therapeutic approach and may lead to a more honest and authentic engagement with the person.[47]

One offender experiencing judicial monitoring at the Portland Westside Community Court described the experience:

> you saw in me what most people have overlooked and you taught me that not every [judge] read what's on the paper and expects the worst. You actually saw the hurt and pain in my eyes and wanted to help.[48]

This approach accords with the underlying principle of therapeutic jurisprudence which prioritises a focus upon well-being and problem-solving with a legal frame. As Berman and Feinblatt explain, it facilitates a judicial officer being able to examine a case in '3-D'[49] so that the legal issues are not looked at in isolation from a defendant's life or life experience. The judicial officer is able to engage with the defendant through ongoing judicial supervision and tools such as motivational interviewing to try and break the recidivist trap. As Magistrate Fanning from the Neighbourhood Justice Centre explains:

> All the matters that I deal with in the criminal court, where the person pleads guilty, would be finalised very quickly in a standard Magistrates

Court. Here we'd adjourn a matter for a person to be engaged in various services, they are monitored, assisted, encouraged, sometimes cajoled to attend those services and be engaged. So there is judicial support for that process with a view to dealing with the underlying causes of the offending. And I will give a classic example. . . . A middle aged Vietnamese woman charged with and pleaded guilty to drug trafficking. She has a prior offense for drug trafficking for which she received an eighteen-month sentence in the county court. She was paroled and on release committed this new drug trafficking offense while on parole. So she was in deep trouble. You might expect that in another court that she'd probably be sentenced to a further term of imprisonment for her drug trafficking. However, it seems to me that if that was to take place, she'd serve her sentence, come out and commit another offense. . . . So what we're trying to do is actually break that cycle. We go through a process of endeavoring to look at ways we can help.[50]

Judge Calabrese from the Red Hook Community Justice Center has made a similar observation about the judicial officer's role within the model:

As a judge working in a traditional courtroom, I was like a plumber with one tool or an artist with two colors; jail or out. That wasn't effective. Now that I sit at the Red Hook Community Justice Center, I can bring many more tools. I can bring counseling sessions. I can bring community restitution projects, And I can bring anger management classes. I know these kinds of alternative interventions are not appropriate for every case. . . . I've got a real chance at getting at the root cause of the offender's problems so the person doesn't come back before me again and again.[51]

One of the concerns with the model is whether the close connection with the community and interaction with caseworkers impairs the judicial officer's ability to operate independently and impartially while at the same time compromising the court's authority.[52] Feinblatt and Berman observe that this can be a complex 'balancing act' for the judicial officer when it is not the place of the judge 'to manage community relations'.[53] This issue is further explored in Chapter 4.

Training of judicial personnel with the necessary skill set is an issue taken up further in Chapter 4 as it is something that has frequently been identified as a risk in problem-oriented courts more generally. For example, Thompson has noted in the drug court context:

The judges are armed with only limited information. They typically do not have the sort of professional or specialized training that one would expect from someone vested with the responsibility to choose and design treatment programs. Instead, they function on the belief that they can fully understand a defendant's problems sufficiently to dictate what is the best treatment. Judges may become personally invested in the success of a defendant's efforts. In the event of failure, the judge may react personally and increase punishment inappropriately.[54]

One of the issues that the single judge model can present is the difficulty for the Centre of a new judge transitioning into the role as they cultivate the strong community relationships and local knowledge previously held by the former judicial officer.[55] As Chief Judge Satterfield from Washington has explained, 'These projects can't be personality based – they won't be successful in the long term',[56] but at the same time it is often the personality of the judicial officer which sets the tone for the Centre and its interactions. For this reason, managing the complexities associated with the appointment of a new judge is something that the Centre needs to be particularly attuned to.

Collecting data, collecting stories

To ensure ongoing funding and the extension of pilot projects, the continuous collection of data by Community Justice Centres have proved to be essential. Without data and stories of success it is difficult for staff to show justice agencies that the Centre's resource spend is justified and achieving its goals. The data collation itself is resource intensive and requires staffing, time and planning.

However, what has also proven a challenge for Community Justice Centres is finding ways that their activities can be evaluated when the standard criminal justice indicators of recidivism, time between offences and severity of offending do not capture the depth of the community engagement, crime prevention and success in addressing underlying criminogenic factors. While it is the community which becomes a big part of a study of a Community Justice Centre, separating out what improvement can be attributed back to the Centre and what may stem from changes in policing, employment cycles or gentrification is not always straightforward. The complexity of managing Community Justice Centre evaluations and the need for bespoke evaluation approaches are outlined further in Chapter 4.

Community planning

Community justice begins and ends with neighborhoods.[57]

For Community Justice Centres, designing the Centre in partnership with the local neighbourhood is imperative.[58] This is a multifaceted process which requires an open discussion at the grassroots level about community need but also gauges community support for initiatives.[59] For the Red Hook Community Justice Center the community and a broad range of stakeholders was involved throughout, even in selecting the old school to house it. The relationship with the community was developed through initial work with the Public Safety Corps which created buy-in and trust in the Center at the very outset. The Corps would help locals with their shopping or public housing issues and ask for local input in how to improve Red Hook.[60] Some perceived failings in the planning of the North Liverpool Community Justice Centre proved to be critical to how the Centre was received by residents across the four communities it served.[61] For the Harlem Community Justice Center it was these early discussions and focus groups which drove and ultimately redirected the Centre's concentration:

> Our assumption when we started planning a community court in Harlem was that we'd adopt the model of the Midtown Community Court . . . but the more we talked to people the more we discovered folks weren't really talking about graffiti, public urination, turnstile-jumping the way they were in Midtown just a few miles away. . . . They were interested in the impact drugs were having on young people, and housing issues, like landlord-tenant problems and the lack of affordable housing.[62]

Conclusion

The experiment of Community Justice has over the last three decades introduced novel justice approaches which have altered the relationship between the courts and the community. Lanni identifies that it has found both 'support and resistance on both sides of the political spectrum' when:

> Conservatives have lauded the aggressive enforcement of quality of life offenses as a way to clean up troubled neighborhoods. However, some conservatives have also criticized problem-solving courts as rehabilitation at the expense of accountability and individual responsibility. . . . [L]iberals have raised concerns of their own that some programs would encroach on civil liberties by encouraging arrests for minor offenses and coercing offenders into guilty pleas and treatment without adequate adversarial procedures. Nevertheless, many liberals have also found attractive the notion of community participation and empowerment central to the community justice movement. They have also approved of its emphasis on treatment, the provision of social services, and offender reintegration in place of incarceration.[63]

This conflict in the movement's reception reflects tensions within the criminal justice system itself, tensions which Community Justice Centres have sought to find ways to overcome.

Notes

1 Greg Berman, *Principles of Community Justice – A Guide for Community Court Planners* (Center for Court Innovation, 2010) 2.
2 Ibid. 58.
3 Neighbourhood Justice Centre, 'Reflections on Practice: The First Six Years', 2012, 38, www.neighbourhoodjustice.vic.gov.au/sites/default/files/embridge_cache/emshare/original/public/2020/04/41/aa45f4d34/njc%2Breflections%2Bin%2Bpractice%20%281%29.pdf
4 Margaret Jackson, William Glackman and Christopher Giles, 'Downtown Community Court Participant Survey II', 2012, 141, https://www2.gov.bc.ca/assets/gov/law-crime-and-justice/courthouse-services/community-court/dcc-research-compilation.pdf
5 Neighbourhood Justice Centre, 'Embedded Specialist Support Services', www.neighbourhoodjustice.vic.gov.au/knowledge-centre/our-model/embedded-specialist-support-services
6 Margaret Jackson et al., 'Compilation of Research on the Vancouver Downtown Community Court 2008 to 2012', 2012, 32, https://www2.gov.bc.ca/assets/gov/law-crime-and-justice/courthouse-services/community-court/dcc-research-compilation.pdf
7 M. Somjen Frazer, *The Impact of the Community Court Model on Defendant Perceptions of Fairness: A Case Study at the Red Hook Community Justice Center* (Center for Court Innovation, 2006) 24, www.courtinnovation.org/sites/default/files/Procedural_Fairness.pdf
8 Judge Alex Calabrese, 'Red Hook Community Justice Center', www.courtinnovation.org/publications/alex-calabrese-judge-red-hook-community-justice-center
9 See, e.g. Cynthia G. Lee et al., *A Community Court Grows in Brooklyn: A Comprehensive Evaluation of the Red Hook Community Justice Center – Final Report* (National Center for State Courts, 2013) 64.
10 North Integrated Family Violence Services Partnership, 'Neighbourhood Justice Centre', November 2017, www.nifvs.org.au/resources/case-studies/the-neighbourhood-justice-centre/
11 Robin Steinberg and Skyla Albertson, 'Broken Windows Policing and Community Courts: An Unholy Alliance' (2016) 37 *Cardozo Law Review* 995, 1016.
12 Greg Berman and John Feinblatt, *Good Courts – The Case for Problem-Solving Justice* (New York Press, 2005) 64.
13 Stuart Ross et al., 'Evaluation of the Neighbourhood Justice Centre, City of Yarra Final Report' (2009), 123.
14 Julius Lang, *What Is a Community Court? How the Model Is Being Adapted Across the United States* (Bureau of Justice Assistance, 2011) 12, www.courtinnovation.org/publications/what-community-court-how-model-being-adapted-across-united-states
15 Center for Court Innovation, 'UPNEXT', www.courtinnovation.org/programs/upnext

16   Anthony Morgan and Rick Brown, 'Estimating the Costs Associated with Community Justice' (2015) 507 *Trends & Issues in Crime and Criminal Justice* 10, www.aic.gov.au/media_library/publications/tandi_pdf/tandi507.pdf

17   Margaret Jackson et al., 'Compilation of Research on the Vancouver Downtown Community Court 2008 to 2012', 2012, 35, https://www2.gov.bc.ca/assets/gov/law-crime-and-justice/courthouse-services/community-court/dcc-research-compilation.pdf

18   David R. Karp and Todd R. Clear, 'Community Justice: A Conceptual Framework' (2000) 2 *Criminal Justice* 323; Cynthia G. Lee et al., *A Community Court Grows in Brooklyn: A Comprehensive Evaluation of the Red Hook Community Justice Center – Final Report – Executive Summary* (National Centre for State Courts, 2013) 5.

19   Robert Weidner, *Hartford Community Court: Origins, Expectations and Implementation* (Bureau of Justice Assistance, 1999) 2.

20   Lang, *What Is a Community Court?* above n 14, 12.

21   Neighbourhood Justice Centre, 'Family Safety Services', www.neighbourhoodjustice.vic.gov.au/knowledge-centre/our-service-innovation/family-safety-services

22   Lang, *What Is a Community Court?* above n 14, 2.

23   Ibid.

24   Sarah Schweig, *Beyond a Single Neighborhood* (Center for Court Innovation, 2014) 3–4.

25   Berman, *Principles of Community Justice*, above n 1, 8.

26   Downtown Community Court, 'Downtown Community Court Guiding Principles', https://www2.gov.bc.ca/gov/content/justice/criminal-justice/vancouver-downtown-community-court/how-the-court-works/guiding-principles

27   Calabrese, 'Red Hook Community Justice Center', above n 8.

28   Diana Karafin, 'Community Courts Across the Globe: A Survey of Goals, Performance Measures and Operations', 2008, 7, www.courtinnovation.org/sites/default/files/community_court_world.pdf

29   Neighbourhood Justice Centre, 'Community-based Crime Prevention: Theory and Practice' (undated).

30   Lang, *What Is a Community Court?* above n 14, 9.

31   Adriaan Lanni, 'The Future of Community Justice' (2005) Summer *Harvard Civil Rights – Civil Liberties Law Review* 359, 380.

32   Sarah Murray and Harry Blagg, 'Reconceptualising Community Justice Centre Evaluations – Lessons from the North Liverpool Experience' (2018) 27(2) *Griffith Law Review* 1.

33   Greg Berman and David Anderson, *Engaging the Community: A Guide for Community Justice Planners* (Bureau of Justice Assistance & Centre for Court Innovation, 3rd edn, 2010) 5.

34   Downtown Community Court Executive Board, 'Report from the DCC Executive Board on the Final Evaluation of the Downtown Community Court', 2013, 10, https://www2.gov.bc.ca/assets/gov/law-crime-and-justice/courthouse-services/community-court/dcc-evaluation-executive-board.pdf

35   Tyrell A. Connor, 'Legitimation in Action: An Examination of Community Courts and Procedural Justice' (2018) *Journal of Crime and Justice* 1, 19–20. See generally, Tom Tyler, *Why People Obey the Law* (Princeton University Press, 1990); Tom Tyler (ed), *Procedural Justice* (Ashgate, 2005); John Thibaut

and Laurens Walker, *Procedural Justice: A Psychological Analysis* (Lawrence Erlbaum Associates, 1975); Tom Tyler, 'Citizen Discontent With Legal Procedures: A Social Science Perspective on Civil Procedure Reform' (1997) 45 *American Journal of Comparative Law* 871; Kevin Burke and Steve Leben, 'Procedural Fairness: A Key Ingredient in Public Satisfaction' (2007–2008) 44 *Court Review* 4, 7, http://aja.ncsc.dni.us/courtrv/cr44-1/CR44-1-2BurkeLeben. pdf

36 Lee et al., *A Community Court Grows in Brooklyn – Executive Summary*, above n 18, 10.

37 Margaret Jackson and William Glackman, 'Downtown Community Court Phase I Participant Survey: Final Report', 2010, 116, https://www2.gov.bc.ca/assets/gov/law-crime-and-justice/courthouse-services/community-court/dcc-research-compilation.pdf

38 Ross et al., 'Evaluation of the Neighbourhood Justice Centre, City of Yarra Final Report', above n 13, 123.

39 Lee et al., *A Community Court Grows in Brooklyn – Final Report*, above n 9, Appendix A, 39–40.

40 Ibid., Appendix A, 42.

41 Robert V. Wolf, 'Community Justice Around the Globe: An International Overview' (2006) July/August *Crime and Justice International* 4, 11.

42 See, e.g. Lanni, 'The Future of Community Justice', above n 31. But cf., John Feinblatt and Greg Berman, 'Community Courts: A Brief Primer' (2001) January *United States Attorney's Bulletin* 33, 37.

43 George Mair and Matthew Millings, *Doing Justice Locally: The North Liverpool Community Justice Centre* (Centre for Crime and Justice Studies, 2011) 76, https://assets.justice.vic.gov.au/njc/resources/488e89e5-f5ac-4c73-a4e6-e32236e1bb1c/doing_justice_locally_northliverpool.pdf

44 Anita Barraud, 'One-Stop Legal Shop', *The Law Report – ABC Radio National*, 3 April 2007, www.abc.net.au/radionational/programs/lawreport/one-stop-legal-shop/3400580

45 Frazer, *The Impact of the Community Court Model on Defendant Perceptions of Fairness*, above n 7, 24.

46 Elizabeth Richardson, *Innovative Approaches to Justice: The NJC Experience – Sentencing Approaches* (ACJI, 2013) 10, www.monash.edu/__data/assets/pdf_file/0004/946831/Module-3_Background-materials-styled.pdf

47 Ibid. 13.

48 Greg Berman and John Feinblatt, *Good Courts – The Case for Problem-Solving Justice* (New York Press, 2005) 89.

49 Ibid. 34.

50 Neighbourhood Justice Centre, 'Reflections on Practice', above n 3, 43.

51 Greg Berman and Aubrey Fox, 'From the Margins to the Mainstream: Community Justice at the Crossroads" (2001) 22(2) *Justice System Journal* 189, 193 (Judge Alex Calabrese).

52 See, e.g. Anthony Thompson, 'Courting Disorder: Some Thoughts on Community Courts' court judicial officers).

53 John Feinblatt and Greg Berman, 'Community Courts: A Brief Primer' (2001) January *United States Attorney's Bulletin* 33, 36.

54 Ibid. 79.

55 Sarah Murray, 'Keeping It in the Neighbourhood? Neighbourhood Courts in the Australian Context' (2009) 35(1) *Monash University Law Review* 74, 92.

56 Schweig, *Beyond a Single Neighborhood*, above n 24, 3.
57 Berman and Anderson, *Engaging the Community*, above n 33, 3.
58 Ibid.
59 Leslie Paik, *Surveying Communities – A Resource for Community Justice Planners* (Bureau of Justice Assistance, 2003).
60 Calabrese, 'Red Hook Community Justice Center', above n 8. Alex Calabrese, 'The Impact of Problem Solving Courts on the Lawyer's Role and Ethics' (2002) 29 *Fordham Urban Law Journal* 1892, 1912.
61 Murray and Blagg, 'Reconceptualising Community Justice Centre Evaluations', above n 32, 5.
62 Robert V. Wolf, *Defining the Problem Using Data to Plan a Community Justice Project* (Centre for Court Innovation, 1999) 1 quoting Rodney Sprauve.
63 Lanni, 'The Future of Community Justice', above n 31, 368–9.

Bibliography

Barraud, Anita. 'One-Stop Legal Shop', 3 April 2007, www.abc.net.au/radionational/programs/lawreport/one-stop-legal-shop/3400580

Berman, Greg. *Principles of Community Justice – A Guide for Community Court Planners* (Center for Court Innovation, 2010).

Berman, Greg and David Anderson. *Engaging the Community: A Guide for Community Justice Planners* (Bureau of Justice Assistance & Centre for Court Innovation, 3rd edn, 2010).

Berman, Greg and John Feinblatt. *Good Courts – The Case for Problem-Solving Justice* (New York Press, 2005).

Berman, Greg and Aubrey Fox. 'From the Margins to the Mainstream: Community Justice at the Crossroads' (2001) 22(2) *Justice System Journal* 189.

Burke, Kevin and Steve Leben. 'Procedural Fairness: A Key Ingredient in Public Satisfaction' (2007–2008) 44 *Court Review* 4, http://aja.ncsc.dni.us/courtrv/cr44-1/CR44-1-2BurkeLeben.pdf

Calabrese, Alex. 'Red Hook Community Justice Center', www.courtinnovation.org/publications/alex-calabrese-judge-red-hook-community-justice-center

Calabrese, Alex. 'The Impact of Problem Solving Courts on the Lawyer's Role and Ethics' (2002) 29 *Fordham Urban Law Journal* 1892.

Center for Court Innovation. 'UPNEXT', www.courtinnovation.org/programs/upnext

Connor, Tyrell A. 'Legitimation in Action: An Examination of Community Courts and Procedural Justice' (2018) *Journal of Crime and Justice* 1.

Downtown Community Court. 'Downtown Community Court Guiding Principles', https://www2.gov.bc.ca/gov/content/justice/criminal-justice/vancouver-downtown-community-court/how-the-court-works/guiding-principles

Downtown Community Court Executive Board. 'Report from the DCC Executive Board on the Final Evaluation of the Downtown Community Court', 2013, https://www2.gov.bc.ca/assets/gov/law-crime-and-justice/courthouse-services/community-court/dcc-evaluation-executive-board.pdf

Feinblatt, John and Greg Berman. 'Community Courts: A Brief Primer' (2001) January *United States Attorney's Bulletin* 33.

Frazer, M. Somjen. *The Impact of the Community Court Model on Defendant Perceptions of Fairness: A Case Study at the Red Hook Community Justice Center* (Center for Court Innovation, 2006), www.courtinnovation.org/sites/default/files/ Procedural_Fairness.pdf

Jackson, Margaret and William Glackman. 'Downtown Community Court Phase I Participant Survey: Final Report', 2010, 116, https://www2.gov.bc.ca/assets/ gov/law-crime-and-justice/courthouse-services/community-court/dcc-research-compilation.pdf

Jackson, Margaret, William Glackman and Christopher Giles. 'Downtown Community Court Participant Survey II', 2012, https://www2.gov.bc.ca/assets/ gov/law-crime-and-justice/courthouse-services/community-court/dcc-research-compilation.pdf

Jackson, Margaret et al. 'Compilation of Research on the Vancouver Downtown Community Court 2008 to 2012', 2012, https://www2.gov.bc.ca/assets/gov/ law-crime-and-justice/courthouse-services/community-court/dcc-research-compilation.pdf

Karafin, Diana. 'Community Courts Across the Globe: A Survey of Goals, Performance Measures and Operations', 2008, www.courtinnovation.org/sites/ default/files/community_court_world.pdf

Karp, David R. and Todd R. Clear. 'Community Justice: A Conceptual Framework' (2000) 2 *Criminal Justice* 323.

Lanni, Adriaan. 'The Future of Community Justice' (2005) Summer *Harvard Civil Rights Civil Liberties Law Review* 359.

Lang, Julius. *What Is a Community Court? How the Model Is Being Adapted Across the United States* (Bureau of Justice Assistance, 2011), www.courtinnovation. org/publications/what-community-court-how-model-being-adapted-across-united-states

Lee, Cynthia G. et al. *A Community Court Grows in Brooklyn: A Comprehensive Evaluation of the Red Hook Community Justice Center – Final Report- Executive Summary* (National Centre for State Courts, 2013).

Lee, Cynthia G. et al. *A Community Court Grows in Brooklyn: A Comprehensive Evaluation of the Red Hook Community Justice Center – Final Report* (National Centre for State Courts, 2013).

Mair, George and Matthew Millings. *Doing Justice Locally: The North Liverpool Community Justice Centre* (Centre for Crime and Justice Studies, 2011), https:// assets.justice.vic.gov.au/njc/resources/488e89e5-f5ac-4c73-a4e6-e32236e1bb1c/ doing_justice_locally_northliverpool.pdf

Morgan, Anthony and Rick Brown. 'Estimating the Costs Associated with Community Justice' (2015) 507 *Trends & Issues in Crime and Criminal Justice*, www.aic. gov.au/media_library/publications/tandi_pdf/tandi507.pdf

Murray, Sarah. 'Keeping It in the Neighbourhood? Neighbourhood Courts in the Australian Context' (2009) 35(1) *Monash University Law Review* 74.

Murray, Sarah and Harry Blagg. 'Reconceptualising Community Justice Centre Evaluations – Lessons from the North Liverpool Experience' (2018) 27(2) *Griffith Law Review* 1.

Neighbourhood Justice Centre. 'Community-based Crime Prevention: Theory and Practice' (undated).

Neighbourhood Justice Centre. 'Embedded Specialist Support Services', www.neighbourhoodjustice.vic.gov.au/knowledge-centre/our-model/embedded-specialist-support-services

Neighbourhood Justice Centre. 'Family Safety Services', www.neighbourhoodjustice.vic.gov.au/knowledge-centre/our-service-innovation/family-safety-services

Neighbourhood Justice Centre. 'Reflections on Practice: The First Six Years', 2012, www.neighbourhoodjustice.vic.gov.au/sites/default/files/embridge_cache/emshare/original/public/2020/04/41/aa45f4d34/njc%2Breflections%2Bin%2Bpractice%20%281%29.pdf

Northern Integrated Family Violence Services. 'Neighbourhood Justice Centre', November 2017, www.nifvs.org.au/resources/case-studies/the-neighbourhood-justice-centre/

Paik, Leslie. *Surveying Communities – A Resource for Community Justice Planners* (Bureau of Justice Assistance, 2003).

Richardson, Elizabeth. *Innovative Approaches to Justice: The NJC Experience – Sentencing Approaches* (ACJI, 2013), www.monash.edu/__data/assets/pdf_file/0004/946831/Module-3_Background-materials-styled.pdf

Ross, Stuart et al. 'Evaluation of the Neighbourhood Justice Centre, City of Yarra Final Report' (2009).

Schweig, Sarah. *Beyond a Single Neighborhood* (Center for Court Innovation, 2014).

Steinberg, Robin and Skyla Albertson. 'Broken Windows Policing and Community Courts: An Unholy Alliance' (2016) 37 *Cardozo Law Review* 995.

Thibaut, John and Laurens Walker. *Procedural Justice: A Psychological Analysis* (Lawrence Erlbaum Associates, 1975).

Thompson, Anthony. 'Courting Disorder: Some Thoughts on Community Courts' (2002) 10 *Washington University Journal of Law and Policy* 63.

Tyler, Tom. *Why People Obey the Law* (Princeton University Press, 1990).

Tyler, Tom. 'Citizen Discontent With Legal Procedures: A Social Science Perspective on Civil Procedure Reform' (1997) 45 *American Journal of Comparative Law* 871.

Tyler, Tom (ed). *Procedural Justice* (Ashgate, 2005).

Weidner, Robert. *Hartford Community Court: Origins, Expectations and Implementation* (Bureau of Justice Assistance, 1999).

Wolf, Robert V. *Defining the Problem Using Data to Plan a Community Justice Project* (Centre for Court Innovation, 1999), 1.

Wolf, Robert V. 'Community Justice Around the Globe: An International Overview' (2006) July/August *Crime and Justice International* 4.

3   Case studies of community justice

Introduction

In this chapter the focus is on four Community Justice Centre case studies: the Red Hook Community Justice Center and the Brownsville Community Justice Center (both in New York City but showcasing quite different
approaches), the Neighbourhood Justice Centre, which services the City of
Yarra, in Victoria, Australia, and some recent Community Justice Centre
initiatives in Israel. These case studies are designed to give the reader a
more detailed sense of how the operation of Community Justice Centres dif-
fers from more mainstream justice environments and how the Centres, far
from being facsimiles of each other, are tailored to their particular community and its particular socio-political context. The case studies also identify
some of the evaluation track records of these Centres.

There are many other Community Justice examples that could have been
outlined here. The model has continued to burgeon across the United States.
Canada is exploring a range of new Community Justice Centres.[1] Similarly,
Scotland has recently opened its first Community Justice exemplar with
the Inverness Justice Centre.[2] The four exemplars which are the focus of
this chapter, however, offer four models, which while holding many similar
characteristics, demonstrate distinct approaches.

Red Hook Community Justice Center

The tragic beginnings of the Red Hook Community Justice Center is a story
often repeated. A local school principal, Patrick Daly, was caught up in a
gang shoot-out and was killed. It put in train a series of planning processes
to try and turn the area around which eventually saw the doors of the Justice Center open in 2000. As Berman and Fox explained, it represented an
opportunity to 'improv[e] the safety of the neighborhood and enhance[e] the
legitimacy of the justice system in the eyes of local residents'.[3] Its location

DOI: 10.4324/9780367823320-3

(the former Visitation School) and the name for the Justice Center arose through working closely to engage community members with the planning process.[4]

The Center houses a court which has the jurisdiction to hear a range of civil and criminal matters. The approach of the court's judge, Judge Alex Calabrese, is to work with defendants by hearing their cases, monitoring their progress and delivering sentences which provide them with supports while giving back to the Red Hook community. One defendant, who recounted being treated at the Center 'as a person, not as a docket number' eventually asked Judge Calabrese to solemnise on her wedding day.[5] The Judge has become well known in the area for his innovations at the court as a judicial officer:

> whose instinctive mode of interaction is a verbal bear hug, [who] sat at eye level with defendants. He congratulated them on each victory, no matter how small. He explained clearly, in plain language. He asked defendants to tell the court how they had ended up there. He quizzed them on their plans for the future.[6]

The approach at the Red Hook Community Justice Center is about 'deterrence, intervention and enhanced legitimacy of the justice system'.[7] This means that the court wants the offender to take responsibility for even minor offences to recognise the impact on victims and the community as well as on their own life, and this can see the court ordering community service to give back for the harm done. By deterring people from continuing to commit crime the court aims to reduce minor offending but also felonies.[8] In contrast to the Midtown Community Court most individuals who come before Judge Calabrese are Red Hook residents.[9] Defence counsel are present for trials and both contested and uncontested matters can be dealt with by the court. Intervention is about using the authority of the court to promote and support individual change through engagement with service supports. There are a number of programs offered through the Center such as a Driver Accountability Program,[10] counselling, vocational training and drug and alcohol rehabilitation.

The Center, based on the ideas of procedural justice and therapeutic jurisprudence, seeks to change an individual's perception of the justice system by treating them with respect, making them feel part of the process and facilitating direct communication between the bench and the individual.

The Red Hook Community is pivotal to the operation of the Center, and Judge Calabrese has a close knowledge of the Red Hook area:

> I also get to know the people who run the community garden, the artists who are moving into the area, and the staff of the local library.

I know the principal at the nearby school, and I know that residents call an apartment building plagued by drug dealing "The Pharmacy". What difference does this make? Because the Justice Center has a better understanding of the community and its problems. I can use this knowledge to help craft meaningful and lasting solutions. If I arraign an offender arrested in the Pharmacy or address a housing dispute there, I can formulate a disposition that addresses not only the problem at hand but also the community's long-standing wish to make the building a better place to live.[11]

There is, however, an express intent to keep the court separate from the community so that it can carry out its work with independence and impartiality.[12] This is vital for the community's regard for the Center and public confidence in the court which it houses. This means for instance that the Red Hook community helps design and participates in community programs in the local area but this does not spill over into the court's operations.[13]

The community can take part in the Peacemaking Program which trains local residents to help resolve neighbourhood disagreements or the Bridging the Gap Program which provides opportunities for police to improve connections with local residents.[14] The Red Hook Youth Internship Program or the Youth Court provide innovative ways to engage local youth in the community and aid self-growth. Judge Calabrese describes:

Attend[ing] a hearing where a youth respondent was caught with a box cutter in school. At first he said he was holding it for a friend and the teacher just happened to catch him "at a bad time." Once the members of Youth Court started questioning him – the jury is allowed to ask questions – it became clear that he took the weapon to school with him. Then the jury asked, "Does your little brother look up to you?" The respondent answered, "Yes." The jury asked, "Would you want him carrying a box cutter to school?" The respondent answered, "Of course not!" Then the judge asked the clinching question, "If your younger brother sees you take a box cutter to school and he looks up to you, why isn't he going to do the same thing?" You could almost see the respondent start to think about being a role model and the message his behavior sent to his family and the community.[15]

Services can also be accessed generally so 'you don't have to get arrested to get help' whether that be support from the Housing Resource Center or mediation assistance.[16]

Evaluating the Red Hook Community Justice Center involves engagement with the community through a combination of an 'annual door-to-door survey, intermittent focus groups, and day-to-day interactions with court users'.[17] Independent evaluation reports have found that the Center has brought about significant cost savings and reductions in victimisation expenses as well as reducing recidivism by 10% in adults and 20% in youth as against mainstream courts.[18] Some data also suggests that order compliance rates range between 63.7% to 75.5% depending on the measures imposed, including drug rehabilitation and community service.[19] Studies have also found that satisfaction with the Red Hook court process was superior to mainstream courts, and that satisfaction levels diverged to a lesser degree according to 'race and socioeconomic status'.[20] There also many qualitative stories of success, for example:

> Stacey Cornelius, 47, credits the Red Hook courthouse for getting her clean after a 2008 arrest for buying drugs. She was sent upstate for a month of drug rehabilitation and then sentenced to another nine months of intensive, four times-per-week counselling that, if she missed, would result in a year of jail. She says she's been sober ever since. "He helped me to do what I was supposed to do," she said of Judge Calabrese. "Now I'm just focused on me."[21]

As Judge Calabrese notes, '[b]y having a presence in the community, I think we can really make great strides in lowering crime and making it a better place to live'.[22]

Neighbourhood Justice Centre

The seed for the Neighbourhood Justice Centre was sown following the Victorian Attorney-General Rob Hulls's visit to the Red Hook Community Justice Center in 2004. Hulls explained that, while visiting Red Hook:

> a woman came before the judge who had been in contact with the court when her son was up on various drug charges. Upon questioning the young man and his family, the judge discovered that the boy's mother also had an addiction. Although the woman had not been charged, the judge drove home the importance of her own rehabilitation to her son's recovery and she agreed to undergo treatment. Returning before the court, she reported an incredibly positive turn around, an enrolment in a counselling course and an optimistic future for both her and her son . . .
> I returned inspired and determined, then, to see what we could do in Victoria to increase creativity and local participation in the law and, in consultation across the legal system, decided to establish a Victorian form of neighbourhood justice – one that drew its strength and authority from the participation of a ready, able and willing community.[23]

Hulls embarked on a local campaign to garner support from local stakeholders for a new Victorian centre in Collingwood in the City of Yarra which was close to the city of Melbourne and which had well over double the crime rate of other areas in the State.[24] Two years later the *Courts Legislation (Neighbourhood Justice Centre) Act 2006* (Vic) (the Act) was passed to provide legislative scaffolding for the 'Neighbourhood Justice Division'.[25] The Centre opened in early 2007 in a renovated but disused technical college building.

The goals of the Centre were to improve community safety and justice indicators while also changing the local community's relationship with justice agencies such that the Centre 'draws its strength and authority from the participation' of the neighbourhood housing it.[26] The Centre has avoided the dominance of the courtroom by 'hiding' it on the floor above the lobby such that:

> people who use the Centre for non-court related activities do not disturb court, and equally, do not feel like they are in a courthouse. It also alleviates the need for clients of the court to congregate on the street.[27]

This is aided by a welcoming environment with a children's play area, local art displayed throughout the building and a more dynamic court security which has avoided the use of airport-like security scanners. The first Director of the Centre described how:

> a visitor pointed out to me that it was the first court she'd been in the state where the loudspeaker wasn't used to call the person's name out. In fact, here the person is approached and told it is time to go in. And what a change that made in the dynamic. It's small but it was a conscious decision when we started to not use the public address system. That's one of the reasons we have the concierge function built into security.[28]

The Centre has a staff member called the 'Neighbourhood Justice Officer' who supports visitors to the Centre, provides assistance to those appearing before the court and also runs 'problem-solving meetings'[29] as an 'out-of-court process'[30] either for community members or following court-referral.

The Neighbourhood Justice Centre's Magistrate, David Fanning, was chosen by a panel which included community members,[31] with this appointment being required by the Act to have regard to the appointee's familiarity with therapeutic jurisprudence and restorative justice.[32] The Court hears criminal matters both for adults and children (excluding sexual offences and committals for indictable offences) as well as family violence cases (heard once-weekly),[33] matters before the Victims of Crime Assistance Tribunal and civil matters including housing and guardianship through its Victorian Civil and Administrative Tribunal jurisdiction. It has jurisdiction to hear cases where the defendant lives in the City of Yarra, is homeless but is residing in the City of Yarra (or committed the offence in the area) or if an Aboriginal person has a 'close connection' with the area to which the criminal charge relates.[34] Matters which do not meet these criteria or which are contested can be referred to other courts.

While not all matters require it, the Magistrate is able to defer matters to allow defendants to engage with the Client Services team and can take advice in open court from this team in crafting order conditions or sentences.[35] The Client Services Team includes caseworkers with expertise in drug and alcohol addiction, family violence, employment assistance, housing support, mental health and financial counselling.[36] The Centre also has a Koori Justice Worker who is available to support Aboriginal visitors to the Centre.[37] One team-member commented that:

> [i]t is very much about shifting motivation and saying to clients "next time you will be in court will be on this date and you are in a position to actually act on sentencing and influence the magistrate on sentencing by what you do. So what is it you would like to do?"[38]

The place-based support can ensure that defendants get assistance more readily and in a way that can be integrated in a bespoke fashion. Sentencing deferrals or matter adjournments ensure that the defendant is placed on an order at a point when success is more likely, rather than receiving a community order when personal circumstances such as homelessness or addiction are likely to obstruct compliance with the order's terms. Judicial supervision monitors a defendant's readiness as well as seeking to motivate the defendant to begin to tackle some of the challenges at the root of their offending behaviour.

The Client Services Team are also housed alongside police prosecutors, defence lawyers and corrections staff, and there are confidentiality and case management protocols in place to govern interactions:

> with client permission, [Client Services staff] do a handover meeting with Corrections. We work out the little indicators that the professionals need to pick up on if the client is losing focus and also to leave the door open for us to be called in again if necessary.[39]

It is also the case that sentences like Community Correction Orders (CCOs) are collaboratively designed, with the Magistrate:

> seeking input from the person about optional conditions, and then before a CCO is imposed, obtain[ing] a report from Community Corrections containing their recommendations for appropriate conditions. In their assessment of the person, Community Corrections will explain judicial monitoring and other conditions to the person. Magistrate Fanning will again explain the process in court and seek the person's agreement to comply with the conditions of the order. It is his experience that people generally attend judicial monitoring reviews because they feel an obligation to come to court even if they may not be complying with other conditions.[40]

The Neighbourhood Justice Centre describes how, '[t]he offender is monitored, encouraged and sometimes cajoled to attend services. In all, the person receives judicial support to walk the path to healing and reform'.[41] In one case study it notes how:

> [a] young man before court had a range of charges and a host of complex psycho-social problems. Our Magistrate deferred his sentence so that Client Services could prioritise his needs. At the time he was resistant to help – he would talk the talk, but not walk the walk.
>
> During his deferral he had a Problem Solving Meeting which had a profound effect on him. As he told his case worker later, he'd never had so many people put so much effort into helping him. He was sentenced to a community-based order during which he worked with NJC's mental health worker. He's now actively handling his treatment plan, and requesting help in a number of other areas in his life.[42]

The Centre has also partnered with the Koori community to introduce measures like an Aboriginal Hearing Day each month which has ensured that key services can be on-site and which seeks to improve the experience of the justice system for Aboriginal defendants.[43]

While the Act requires matters to be conducted with 'as little formality and technicality' as is appropriate,[44] procedural fairness, independence and impartiality are maintained by mechanisms such as the Magistrate not communicating about matters with the co-located staff outside of court time and also being aware of the community relationship. As

Magistrate David Fanning from the Neighbourhood Justice Centre has explained:

> [s]ome people argue and some people believe that the community involvement will undermine the integrity and independence of the neighbourhood justice centre and the court in particular. From my perspective, there's absolutely no evidence to support that.[45]

The Program Innovations Team at the Neighbourhood Justice Centre leads the Centre's work in justice innovation, determining community needs and promoting understanding and adoption of the model. It engages with the City of Yarra community and key stakeholders in developing and delivering its programs. This can include workshops and community education or more long-term programs such as the Collingwood All Stars Soccer Program which brings together police, young people and Centre staff to bring about positive change in local youth through engagement with the program.[46] They have also championed initiatives like the Smith Street Working Group which arose out of tensions between members of the Aboriginal community, police and businesses around Smith Street in Collingwood. Through extensive problem-solving, coming together and relationship building there was an improvement in safety and relations, and it led to initiatives such as the Smith Street Dreaming music festival.[47] The Team also champions reform initiatives to improve the court experience for community members and mentors other courts exploring new justice approaches, as part of the Neighbourhood Justice Centre's role as an International Mentor Community Court.[48] For example, the team designed and piloted an 'online Family Violence Intervention application form' which has subsequently been rolled out across Victoria.[49] The team also provides the Neighbourhood Justice Centre's Peacemaking Service which was inspired by the service at Red Hook.

The Centre has been extensively evaluated since 2007. These evaluations have included savings of $4.56 million/year in avoided prison days, 17% lower rates of re-offending within a two-year time frame compared with other Victorian courts, improvements in order completion and deeper engagement with service agencies.[50] The crime rate in the City of Yarra has significantly declined, although evaluations have recognised that not all improvements can solely be associated with the area's experiment with community justice.[51] Magistrate Fanning has indicated that 'I'm not Pollyanna or starry eyed, but it is very evident that a lot of people have had their lives changed by their association with the NJC'.[52] Evaluations have also found that participants have positive things to say about their justice experience at the Centre:

> There is strong evidence that there are higher levels of confidence by justice system participants at the NJC and that this in turn generates higher levels of meaningful involvement in justice processes. NJC court users report very high levels of satisfaction across a range of measures of court performance and contrast their experiences at the NJC favourably with their experiences at other court venues.[53]

Following an evaluation of the Centre, one defendant commented:

> I was very impressed with the proceedings at NJC. I felt heard and supported in every way and the staff I dealt with were unfailingly polite, friendly and very helpful. I think this kind of court is a fantastic community facility.[54]

Brownsville Community Justice Center

Brownsville Community Justice Center was initially intended to replicate the Red Hook Community Justice Center. Based deep in east Brooklyn, the Center's planned multimillion dollar courthouse[55] did not eventuate. What emerged as a result was the creation of the Brownsville Community Justice Center in the absence of the standard co-located court.

In establishing this newly envisioned model, the Center partnered with the Brownsville neighbourhood. Brownsville had been described as the 'deadliest neighborhood in New York City'[56] with high rates of unemployment and criminal justice system engagement along with significant incidences of murder, drugs and gun use.[57] One survey of locals in 2010 found that community safety was perceived to be an issue more for outsiders than for those from the Brownsville area as 'everyone knows everybody else' but that resident – police relationships were a particular source of tension.[58] It also found that 26% of those surveyed could not identify something that was a 'strength in the community'.[59] When the Community Justice Centre concept was initially floated there was strong support for it.[60] There was a need to ensure that, in transforming the area, it also made local residents feel that they still belonged. The planners took seriously the importance of co-designing the Center with local residents.[61] Similarly, all of its core projects such as rejuvenated youth spaces and community areas have been physically designed and built by Brownsville residents so that they buy in to, and have ownership of, them.

The Brownsville model has been described as facilitating 'multiple off-ramps' for those trapped in a recidivist cycle by providing supports throughout residents' engagement with the justice system—both at the point of entry and as they exit, to lead to a more 'law-abiding' path.[62] This includes Legal Hand, which provides legal information and referrals with locals volunteering to help other residents, as well as the Housing Resource Center, which helps Brownsvillers who are homeless or at risk of homelessness. Its Anti-Violence Project works with offenders who are on parole[63] and seeks to change the culture around gun violence,[64] while its Leadership Project seeks to divert young offenders who live locally into employment, counselling, internships and training opportunities.[65] It also showcases a Learning Lab which provides equipment, training and space for young people.[66] The Center looks for ways to upskill locals and provide them with career paths previously out of reach. As Ionna Jimenez says, '[w]e put cameras in their hands, sewing machines in their hands, software and technology'.[67]

Although it lacks a New York State courthouse it does run a diversionary Youth Court program which trains local youth to hear weekly cases involving young people diverted from mainstream justice channels.[68] Offenders are encouraged to work with support services as well as complete restorative sanctions which they do at a rate of over 90%.[69]

The Center has also embarked on a large local restoration project: the Belmont Revitalization Project which has seen volunteers work to restore and improve the local neighbourhood with murals, improve street lighting and creating more green space and meeting places for community members.[70] A group of young people also worked together to create a youth space in a disused shipping container by setting it up on an empty block in the area.[71]

The Brownsville Community Justice Center provides a particularly interesting example of how the model can change to meet community need, circumstances and stakeholder support. It has run community festivals, helped locals to redesign their surrounds and helped to create a video-game based on living in Brownsville.[72] The development of a standalone Justice Center without the presence of a court has the potential to transform residents' experience of such centres, particularly in locales like Brownsville which houses a juvenile detention facility and where there has been a traditionally antagonistic court–community relationship. While the model has often allowed residents to access a Centre's services without the need to be coming before the Centre's courthouse, the separation of the Brownsville site from a city courthouse may aid the willingness of Brownsville locals to engage with the Centre and its services when surveyed residents have shown a lack of faith in court structures.[73]

Israeli community courts

Be'er-Sheva Magistrates' Court was the first Community Justice Centre set up in Israel in 2014 with others following at the Ramle Magistrates Court and the Tel Aviv Magistrates' Court.[74] Be'er-Sheva, Ramle and Tel Aviv are cities of over 200,000, 70,000 and 400,000 inhabitants respectively.[75] The Israeli model comprises a small Community Court team including a Magistrate, program coordinator, social worker and relevant defence, probation and prosecutorial staff and which holds team meetings and collaborates with a community-based advisory group.[76] A relatively small number of cases are assigned (very serious offences are ineligible) to the Centres following a court hearing and probationary officer review process if the prosecutorial and defence team agree on suitability.[77] Referral is primarily based on whether the offence demonstrates an underlying issue that the Community Court can assist with such as drug or alcohol addiction, aggression/family violence or social issues, particularly where recidivism is an issue and a period of incarceration likely.[78]

Each Community Court participant has a treatment plan prepared and, after pleading guilty, is required to complete the assigned steps and attend relevant appointments. Team meetings allow the community court team to discuss a participant's progress in their absence and discuss team recommendations and differences of opinion.[79] The program coordinator, in a similar way to many drug court programs, plays a particularly key role in coordinating the interdisciplinary team but also guiding the program participant.[80]

Court hearings to supervise progress are conducted in accordance with therapeutic jurisprudential and motivational interviewing principles and see the bench conversing openly with the defendant;[81] however researchers have observed the court process to be more emotionally restrained than some comparative Community Justice Centres.[82] Nevertheless, an 'ethic of care' was strongly evident in one ethnographic study recounting instances such as where the judge said to a participant, 'I want to hug you, you are such a wonderful man'.[83]

A sense of community is created through the Centres through social and religious activities, engagement with local business owners, mentoring, social soccer, community members and students volunteering to assist defendants and their families.[84] Participants undertake community work, are assisted with finding jobs locally and also participate in collaborative projects which have included music-based activities or the establishment of a 'community garden'.[85]

Qualitative assessments of the Israeli model have been positive with more quantitative-focused studies yet to be completed.[86] One recent study noted that 'the vast majority of participants experienced the court as a benevolent entity and felt a sense of belonging in the program, at times even pride for being a part of it'.[87] There was particular evidence of the care of the project team in a participant's progress and individual needs: 'Until now, I always felt helpless because no one wanted to listen. This is the first time that I feel someone is interested in what I'm going through and what bothers me'.[88] Another defendant recounted about their experience:

> At the community court they listen to me and help me. I didn't believe the authorities after fighting them for 40 years. Now I no longer fight. I tell them things and they help me in everything. It gave me back my life.[89]

Conclusion

As demonstrated by these four Community Justice Centre case studies, '[c]ommunity-focused courts will assume various forms, depending on the composition of the community and the nature of the problems brought before the courts'.[90] In so doing they have the potential to change peoples' experience of the justice system. They also have the capacity to help other courts adopt Community Justice approaches with some undertaking formal 'court mentor' roles.[91]

The capacity of Community Justice Centres to continue to do things differently is, however, typically contingent on Centres receiving positive independent evaluations which demonstrate their success. It is some of the challenges presented by evaluating these innovative justice models that is the subject of the next chapter, along with some of the most common criticisms that they face.

Notes

1 Ontario Ministry of the Attorney-General, 'Ontario's Plan for Justice Centres', www.attorneygeneral.jus.gov.on.ca/english/justice-centres/
2 Andrew Dixon, 'See Inside Scotland's First Purpose-Built Justice Centre Which Opened Today in Inverness', *The Inverness Courier*, 30 March 2020, www.inverness-courier.co.uk/news/see-inside-the-inverness-justice-centre-which-opened-today-195214/
3 Greg Berman and Aubrey Fox, 'From the Benches and Trenches: Justice in Red Hook' (2005) 26(1) *Justice System Journal* 77, 79.
4 Ibid. 80.
5 Oren Yaniv, 'Red Hook Community Court Is a Success for Defendants and Taxpayers, Study Shows', *New York Daily News*, 12 November 2013, www.nydailynews.com/new-york/brooklyn/red-hook-community-court-success-study-article-1.1513496

6 Tina Rosenberg, 'The Simple Idea That Could Transform US Criminal Justice', *The Guardian*, 23 June 2015, 3.

7 Cynthia Lee et al., *A Community Court Grows in Brooklyn: A Comprehensive Evaluation of the Red Hook Community Justice Center – Final Report* (National Centre for State Courts, 2013) 4.

8 Ibid. 6.

9 David Rottman, 'Community Courts: Prospects and Limits' (1996) *National Institute of Justice Journal* 46, 50.

10 Center for Court Innovation, 'Driver Accountability Program', www. courtinnovation.org/programs/driver-accountability-program

11 Alex Calabrese, 'Neighborhood Justice: The Red Hook Community Justice Center' (2002) 41 *The Judges' Journal* 7, 9.

12 Berman and Fox, 'From the Benches and Trenches', above n 3, 85.

13 Ibid.

14 Center for Court Innovation, 'Red Hook Community Justice Center', www. courtinnovation.org/programs/red-hook-community-justice-center

15 Alex Calabrese, 'Red Hook Community Justice Center', www.courtinnovation. org/publications/alex-calabrese-judge-red-hook-community-justice-center

16 Lee et al., *A Community Court Grows in Brooklyn: A Comprehensive Evaluation of the Red Hook Community Justice Center – Final Report*, above n 7, 64.

17 Berman and Fox, 'From the Benches and Trenches', above n 3, 86.

18 Lee et al., *A Community Court Grows in Brooklyn: A Comprehensive Evaluation of the Red Hook Community Justice Center – Final Report*, above n 7, 176–7.

19 Susan Flynn, 'The Red Hook Community Justice Center: An Evaluation of a Community Court' (2005) 33 *Journal of Psychiatry & Law* 43, 95.

20 M. Somjen Frazer, *The Impact of the Community Court Model on Defendant Perceptions of Fairness: A Case Study at the Red Hook Community Justice Center* (Center for Court Innovation, 2006) IV, www.courtinnovation.org/sites/ default/files/Procedural_Fairness.pdf

21 Associated Press, 'Report: Brooklyn Community Court a National Model', *The Wall Street Journal*, 14 November 2013.

22 Calabrese, 'Red Hook Community Justice Center', above n 15.

23 Rob Hulls, 'Attorney General's Column: Success of Victoria's First Neighbourhood Justice Centre' (2007) 140 *Victorian Bar News* 9.

24 Stuart Ross, 'Evaluating Neighbourhood Justice: Measuring and Attributing Outcomes for a Community Justice Program' (2015) November 499 *Trends & Issues in Crime and Criminal Justice* 3, www.aic.gov.au/media_library/ publications/tandi_pdf/tandi499.pdf

25 The Act amended the *Magistrates' Court Act 1989* (Vic).

26 Neighbourhood Justice Centre, *The Neighbourhood Justice Centre – Community Justice in Action in Victoria* (Neighbourhood Justice Centre, 2007) 2, 32.

27 Neighbourhood Justice Centre, 'Community Justice in Architecture', www. neighbourhoodjustice.vic.gov.au/knowledge-centre/our-service-innovation/ community-justice-in-architecture

28 Neighbourhood Justice Centre, 'Reflections on Practice: The First Six Years', 2012, 33, www.neighbourhoodjustice.vic.gov.au/sites/default/files/embridge_ cache/emshare/original/public/2020/04/41/aa45f4d34/njc%2Breflections%2Bi n%2Bpractice%20%281%29.pdf

29 See, Jay Jordens and Elizabeth Richardson, 'Collaborative Problem Solving in a Community Court Setting' (2014) 23 *Journal of Judicial Administration* 253.

30 Neighbourhood Justice Centre, 'Welcome – Community Justice – Justice System and Citizens Partnering to Make Communities Safe and Prosperous', 3, www.nifvs.org.au/wp-content/uploads/2017/11/Welcome-to-NJC-document. pdf

31 Anita Barraud, 'One-Stop Legal Shop', *The Law Report – ABC Radio National*, 3 April 2007, www.abc.net.au/radionational/programs/lawreport/one-stop-legal-shop/3400580

32 *Magistrates' Court Act 1989* (Vic), s 4M(5)(a).

33 Ibid. s 4O(4).

34 Ibid. s 4O(2)(a).

35 Ibid. s 4Q(2).

36 Neighbourhood Justice Centre, 'Embedded Specialist Support Services', www.neighbourhoodjustice.vic.gov.au/knowledge-centre/our-model/embedded-specialist-support-services

37 See, e.g. Kylie Smith, 'Reflections on the Design, Country and Community Justice at the Neighbourhood Justice Centre' (2018) 27(2) *Griffith Law Review* 202.

38 Neighbourhood Justice Centre, 'Reflections on Practice', above n 28, 45.

39 Ibid. 48.

40 Elizabeth Richardson, *Innovative Approaches to Justice: The NJC Experience – Sentencing Approaches* (ACJI, 2013) 13–14, www.monash.edu/__data/assets/pdf_file/0004/946831/Module-3_Background-materials-styled.pdf

41 Neighbourhood Justice Centre, 'Welcome – Community Justice', above n 30, 2.

42 Ibid.

43 Neighbourhood Justice Centre, 'Reflections on Practice', above n 28, 35.

44 *Magistrates' Court Act 1989* (Vic), s 4M(7).

45 Barraud, 'One-Stop Legal Shop', above n 31, www.abc.net.au/radionational/programs/lawreport/one-stop-legal-shop/3400580

46 Neighbourhood Justice Centre, 'Join Yarra Kids Soccer', www.neighbourhoodjustice.vic.gov.au/our-services/in-our-community/join-yarra-kids-soccer

47 Neighbourhood Justice Centre, 'Neighbourhood Justice Centre, Community-based Crime Prevention: Theory and Practice' (undated) 28–32; Delia O'Donohue (in consultation with the NJC and Smith Street Working Group), 'Smith Street Dreaming', February 2014, http://assets.justice.vic.gov.au/njc/resources/a65c1f63-7568-4d20-92de-6f145bd1a0d8/smith_str_working_group_master.pdf

48 Neighbourhood Justice Centre, 'Strategic Plan 2019–2023', 2019, 8, www.neighbourhoodjustice.vic.gov.au/sites/default/files/embridge_cache/emshare/original/public/2020/04/21/3a7da1bdf/NJC%20Strat%20Plan%202019-2023.pdf

49 Neighbourhood Justice Centre, 'Family Safety Services', www.neighbourhoodjustice.vic.gov.au/knowledge-centre/our-service-innovation/family-safety-services

50 Victorian Auditor-General, 'Managing Community Correction Orders' (2017) 33; Stuart Ross et al., 'Evaluation of the Neighbourhood Justice Centre, City of Yarra- Final Report' (December 2009); Anthony Morgan and Rick Brown, 'Estimating the Costs Associated with Community Justice' (2015) 507 *Trends & Issues in Crime and Criminal Justice*, www.aic.gov.au/media_library/

publications/tandi_pdf/tandi507.pdf. The Centre's funding was extended at the conclusion if its initial pilot by the Victorian Liberal Government.
51 Ross, 'Evaluating Neighbourhood Justice', above n 24, 3–4.
52 Neighbourhood Justice Centre, 'Reflections on Practice', above n 28, 34. See also Mark Halsey and Melissa de Vel-Palumbo, 'Courts as Empathic Spaces: Reflections on the Neighbourhood Justice Centre' (2018) 27(2) *Griffith Law Review* 182, 187–8.
53 Ross et al., *Evaluation of the Neighbourhood Justice Centre*, above n 50, 8.
54 Ibid. 117.
55 Greg Berman, *Advancing Community Justice: The Challenge of Brownsville, Brooklyn* (Center for Court Innovation, 2013) 9, www.courtinnovation.org/publications/advancing-community-justice-challenge-brownsville-brooklyn
56 Kathleen Culliton, 'This Is the Deadliest Neighborhood in New York City', 11 July 2019, https://patch.com/new-york/brownsville/deadliest-neighborhood-new-york-city
57 Berman, *Advancing Community* Justice, above n 55, 3–4.
58 Suvi Hynynen, *Community Perceptions of Brownsville: A Survey of Neighborhood Quality of Life, Safety and Services* (Center for Court Innovation, 2011) 7, www.courtinnovation.org/sites/default/files/documents/Brownsville%20Op%20Data%20FINAL.pdf
59 Ibid. 8.
60 Ibid. 11.
61 Berman, *Advancing Community Justice*, above n 55, 5, 9.
62 Center for Court Innovation, 'Brownsville Community Justice Center: Fact Sheet' (undated).
63 Elise Jensen et al., *The Brownsville Anti-Violence Project – Evaluation Findings* (Center for Court Innovation, 2016), www.courtinnovation.org/publications/brownsville-anti-violence-project-evaluation-findings
64 An evaluation of the project was mixed – and noted the difficulty of controlling the relevant variables and the challenges with the project evaluation – and found that those who participated were less likely to report gun bearing and had an improved sense of the legitimacy of 'law enforcement' (although this decreased over the course of the project) but less faith in police 'effectiveness' (although this did improve slightly over the course of the project for those who participated): Ibid.
65 Centre for Court Innovation, 'Brownsville Community Justice Center: Brownsville Leadership Project: Alternatives to Incarceration' (undated).
66 Brownsville Community Justice Center, 'Brownsville Learning Lab', http://brownsvillejusticecenter.blogspot.com/p/brownsville-learning-lab.html
67 Monica Morales, 'Part Two: Brownsville on the Rise as Belmont Avenue Makes Comeback', *Pix 11*, 28 August 2019, https://pix11.com/2019/08/28/part-two-brownsville-on-the-rise-as-belmont-avenue-makes-comeback/
68 Brownsville Community Justice Center, 'Brownsville Youth Court', http://brownsvillejusticecenter.blogspot.com/p/brownsville-youth-court.html
69 Center for Court Innovation, 'Brownsville Community Justice Center: Fact Sheet', above n 60.
70 Brownsville Community Justice Center, 'Belmont Avenue Revitalization Project', www.courtinnovation.org/sites/default/files/media/document/2018/BELMONT-REVITALIZATION-PROJECT.pdf

71 News 12, 'Shipping Container Becomes Community Center in Brownsville', http://brooklyn.news12.com/story/34773254/shipping-container-becomes-community-center-in-brownsville
72 Chris Ip, 'The Brooklyn Neighborhood Remade as a VR Game', *Engadget*, 21 June 2018, www.engadget.com/2018-06-21-fireflies-a-brownsville-story-vr-project.html
73 Hynynen, *Community Perceptions of Brownsville*, above n 58, 11.
74 Tali Gal and Hadar Dancig-Rosenberg, '"I Am Starting to Believe in the Word 'Justice'": Lessons from an Ethnographic Study on Community Courts' (2020) 68 *American Journal of Comparative Law* 376, 387–8.
75 Tali Gal and Hadar Dancig-Rosenberg, 'Characterizing Community Courts' (2017) 35 *Behavioral Sciences & the Law* 1, 4.
76 Ibid. 5; Gal and Dancig-Rosenberg, '"I Am Starting to Believe in the Word 'Justice'"', above n 74, 388.
77 Gal and Dancig-Rosenberg, '"I Am Starting to Believe in the Word 'Justice'"', above n 74, 388–9. Gal and Dancig-Rosenberg note that it is directed at offenders facing approximately 12–18 months imprisonment for their crimes (Ibid. 404, fn 112).
78 Ibid. 388–9.
79 Ibid. 394.
80 Ibid. 395.
81 Ibid. 392–3, 396–7.
82 Gal and Dancig-Rosenberg, 'Characterizing Community Courts', above n 75, 11, 14–5.
83 Gal and Dancig-Rosenberg, '"I Am Starting to Believe in the Word 'Justice'"', above n 74, 399.
84 Ibid. 392, 401.
85 Ibid. 401.
86 Ibid. fn 114–5.
87 Ibid.
88 Ibid. 400.
89 Almog Ben Zikri, 'New Community Courts in Israel Emphasize Rehabilitation, Not Punishment', *Haaretz*, 15 May 2017, www.haaretz.com/israel-news/.premium-new-community-courts-in-israel-emphasize-rehabilitation-not-punishment-1.5472138
90 David Rottman, 'Community Courts: Prospects and Limits' (1996) *National Institute of Justice Journal* 46, 50.
91 Centre for Court Innovation, 'Mentor Community Courts', www.courtinnovation.org/mentor-community-courts

Bibliography

Journals, reports, books, media and papers

Associated Press. 'Report: Brooklyn Community Court a National Model', *The Wall Street Journal*, 14 November 2013.

Barraud, Anita. 'One-Stop Legal Shop', 3 April 2007, www.abc.net.au/radio national/programs/lawreport/one-stop-legal-shop/3400580

Berman, Greg. *Advancing Community Justice: The Challenge of Brownsville, Brooklyn* (Center for Court Innovation, 2013), www.courtinnovation.org/publications/advancing-community-justice-challenge-brownsville-brooklyn

Berman, Greg and Aubrey Fox. 'From the Benches and Trenches: Justice in Red Hook' (2005) 26(1) *Justice System Journal* 77.

Brownsville Community Justice Center. 'Belmont Avenue Revitalization Project', www.courtinnovation.org/sites/default/files/media/document/2018/BELMONT-REVITALIZATION-PROJECT.pdf

Brownsville Community Justice Center. 'Brownsville Learning Lab', http://brownsvillejusticecenter.blogspot.com/p/brownsville-learning-lab.html

Brownsville Community Justice Center. 'Brownsville Youth Court', http://brownsvillejusticecenter.blogspot.com/p/brownsville-youth-court.html

Calabrese, Alex. 'Neighborhood Justice: The Red Hook Community Justice Center' (2002) 41 *The Judges' Journal* 7.

Calabrese, Alex. 'Red Hook Community Justice Center', www.courtinnovation.org/publications/alex-calabrese-judge-red-hook-community-justice-center

Center for Court Innovation. 'Alex Calabrese, Judge, Red Hook Community Justice Center – Interview', 2005, https://www.courtinnovation.org/publications/alex-calabrese-judge-red-hook-community-justice-center

Centre for Court Innovation. 'Brownsville Community Justice Center: Brownsville Leadership Project: Alternatives to Incarceration' (undated).

Center for Court Innovation. 'Brownsville Community Justice Center: Fact Sheet' (undated).

Center for Court Innovation. 'Driver Accountability Program', www.courtinnovation.org/programs/driver-accountability-program

Centre for Court Innovation. 'Mentor Community Courts', www.courtinnovation.org/mentor-community-courts

Center for Court Innovation. 'Red Hook Community Justice Center', www.courtinnovation.org/programs/red-hook-community-justice-center

Culliton, Kathleen. 'This Is the Deadliest Neighborhood in New York City', 11 July 2019, https://patch.com/new-york/brownsville/deadliest-neighborhood-new-york-city

Dixon, Andrew. 'See Inside Scotland's First Purpose-Built Justice Centre Which Opened Today in Inverness', *The Inverness Courier*, 30 March 2020, www.inverness-courier.co.uk/news/see-inside-the-inverness-justice-centre-which-opened-today-195214/

Flynn, Susan. 'The Red Hook Community Justice Center: An Evaluation of a Community Court' (2005) 33 *Journal of Psychiatry & Law* 43.

Gal, Tali and Hadar Dancig-Rosenberg. 'Characterizing Community Courts' (2017) 35 *Behavioral Sciences & the Law* 1.

Gal, Tali and Hadar Dancig-Rosenberg. '"I Am Starting to Believe in the Word 'Justice'": Lessons from an Ethnographic Study on Community Courts' (2020) 68 *American Journal of Comparative Law* 376.

Halsey, Mark and Melissa de Vel-Palumbo. 'Courts as Empathic Spaces: Reflections on the Neighbourhood Justice Centre' (2018) 27(2) *Griffith Law Review* 182.

Hulls, Rob. 'Attorney General's Column: Success of Victoria's First Neighbourhood Justice Centre' (2007) 140 *Victorian Bar News* 9.

Hynynen, Suvi. *Community Perceptions of Brownsville: A Survey of Neighborhood Quality of Life, Safety and Services* (Center for Court Innovation, 2011), www.courtinnovation.org/sites/default/files/documents/Brownsville%20Op%20Data%20FINAL.pdf

Ip, Chris. 'The Brooklyn Neighborhood Remade as a VR Game', *Engadget*, 21 June 2018, www.engadget.com/2018-06-21-fireflies-a-brownsville-story-vr-project.html

Jensen, Elise et al. *The Brownsville Anti-Violence Project – Evaluation Findings* (Center for Court Innovation, 2016), www.courtinnovation.org/publications/brownsville-anti-violence-project-evaluation-findings

Jordens, Jay and Elizabeth Richardson. 'Collaborative Problem Solving in a Community Court Setting' (2014) 23 *Journal of Judicial Administration* 253.

Lee, Cynthia et al. *A Community Court Grows in Brooklyn: A Comprehensive Evaluation of the Red Hook Community Justice Center* (National Centre for State Courts, 2013).

Morales, Monica. 'Part Two: Brownsville on the Rise as Belmont Avenue Makes Comeback', *Pix 11*, 28 August 2019, https://pix11.com/2019/08/28/part-two-brownsville-on-the-rise-as-belmont-avenue-makes-comeback/

Morgan, Anthony and Rick Brown. 'Estimating the Costs Associated with Community Justice' (2015) 507 *Trends & Issues in Crime and Criminal Justice*, www.aic.gov.au/media_library/publications/tandi_pdf/tandi507.pdf

Neighbourhood Justice Centre. 'Community Justice in Architecture', www.neighbourhoodjustice.vic.gov.au/knowledge-centre/our-service-innovation/community-justice-in-architecture

Neighbourhood Justice Centre. 'Embedded Specialist Support Services', www.neighbourhoodjustice.vic.gov.au/knowledge-centre/our-model/embedded-specialist-support-services

Neighbourhood Justice Centre. 'Family Safety Services', www.neighbourhoodjustice.vic.gov.au/knowledge-centre/our-service-innovation/family-safety-services

Neighbourhood Justice Centre. 'Join Yarra Kids Soccer', www.neighbourhoodjustice.vic.gov.au/our-services/in-our-community/join-yarra-kids-soccer

Neighbourhood Justice Centre. 'Neighbourhood Justice Centre, Community-based Crime Prevention: Theory and Practice' (undated).

Neighbourhood Justice Centre. *The Neighbourhood Justice Centre – Community Justice in Action in Victoria* (Neighbourhood Justice Centre, 2007).

Neighbourhood Justice Centre. 'Reflections on Practice: The First Six Years', 2012, www.neighbourhoodjustice.vic.gov.au/sites/default/files/embridge_cache/emshare/original/public/2020/04/41/aa45f4d34/njc%2Breflections%2Bin%2Bpractice%20%281%29.pdf

Neighbourhood Justice Centre. 'Strategic Plan 2019–2023', 2019, www.neighbourhoodjustice.vic.gov.au/sites/default/files/embridge_cache/emshare/original/public/2020/04/21/3a7da1bdf/NJC%20Strat%20Plan%202019-2023.pdf

Neighbourhood Justice Centre. 'Welcome – Community Justice – Justice System and Citizens Partnering to Make Communities Safe and Prosperous', www.nifvs. org.au/wp-content/uploads/2017/11/Welcome-to-NJC-document.pdf

News 12. 'Shipping Container Becomes Community Center in Brownsville', http://brooklyn.news12.com/story/34773254/shipping-container-becomes-community-center-in-brownsville

O'Donohue, Delia (in consultation with the NJC and Smith Street Working Group). 'Smith Street Dreaming', February 2014, http://assets.justice.vic.gov.au/njc/resources/a65c1f63-7568-4d20-92de-6f145bd1a0d8/smith_str_working_group_master.pdf

Ontario Ministry of the Attorney-General. 'Ontario's Plan for Justice Centres', www.attorneygeneral.jus.gov.on.ca/english/justice-centres/

Richardson, Elizabeth. *Innovative Approaches to Justice: The NJC Experience – Sentencing Approaches* (ACJI, 2013), www.monash.edu/__data/assets/pdf_file/0004/946831/Module-3_Background-materials-styled.pdf

Rosenberg, Tina. 'The Simple Idea That Could Transform US Criminal Justice', *The Guardian*, 23 June 2015, 3.

Ross, Stuart. 'Evaluating Neighbourhood Justice: Measuring and Attributing Outcomes for a Community Justice Program' (2015) November 499 *Trends & Issues in Crime and Criminal Justice*, www.aic.gov.au/media_library/publications/tandi_pdf/tandi499.pdf

Ross, Stuart et al. 'Evaluation of the Neighbourhood Justice Centre, City of Yarra-Final Report' (2009) December.

Rottman, David. 'Community Courts: Prospects and Limits' (1996) *National Institute of Justice Journal* 46.

Smith, Kylie. 'Reflections on the Design, Country and Community Justice at the Neighbourhood Justice Centre' (2018) 27(2) *Griffith Law Review* 202.

Victorian Auditor-General. 'Managing Community Correction Orders' (2017), 33; Stuart Ross et al., 'Evaluation of the Neighbourhood Justice Centre, City of Yarra-Final Report' (2009) December.

Yaniv, Oren. 'Red Hook Community Court Is a Success for Defendants and Taxpayers, Study Shows', *New York Daily News*, 12 November 2013, www.nydailynews.com/new-york/brooklyn/red-hook-community-court-success-study-article-1.1513496

Zikri, Almog Ben. 'New Community Courts in Israel Emphasize Rehabilitation, Not Punishment', *Haaretz*, 15 May 2017, www.haaretz.com/israel-news/.premium-new-community-courts-in-israel-emphasize-rehabilitation-not-punishment-1.5472138

Legislation

Magistrates' Court Act 1989 (Vic).

4 Lessons from community justice

Evaluations, boundaries and obstacles

Introduction

In this chapter some of the challenges presented by Community Justice Centres are unpacked. How can Centres be properly evaluated when their reach is much broader than traditional criminal justice mechanisms? Are the traditional evaluative tools inadequate to convey the 'richness' of Community Justice Centre operations? Does their 'reach' itself present a problem in terms of the service delivery roles that Centres take on while being at the same time wrapped up with the criminal justice system? To what extent do their collaborative processes undermine the traditional independence of the judge? How are Centres to be formed around 'communities' and do they in turn define or contribute to the creation of such groupings? In exploring some of the criticisms of the model, the chapter will assess some of the key obstacles faced by this court innovation and how Centres have responded to them.

Evaluations

The need to demonstrate success is not unique to Community Justice Centres. For any justice reform to be funded, even as a pilot, and to then continue as a line item within the justice budget, its measures will need to be evidence based and supported by independent and sustained evaluations. This is particularly pronounced for the Community Justice Centre model when, depending on how the reform is introduced and where the Centre is housed, front-end costs can be high.[1] However, Community Justice Centres face the additional challenge of needing to demonstrate success when traditional means of doing so are not always apposite.

The issue for Community Justice Centres is delivering improvement across the many channels in which they seek to work, often within short periods of time, and being able to demonstrate this in cost-benefit terms

DOI: 10.4324/9780367823320-4

that make sense to justice bureaucrats. Added to this, quantitative success needs to be married with community traction and legitimacy to ensure that pilots have the necessary institutional goodwill and buy-in to continue to operate within that community. The latter, in turn, can require extensive co-design and community rapport-building which can also absorb a lot of a project budget before the Centre is even off the ground. Tracking qualitative stories of success also needs to be prioritised to ensure the 'real' experience of defendants is not lost in raw data. Finding the right balance for a Centre across these competing imperatives can be no mean feat. As canvassed in Chapter 3, Centres such as the Red Hook Community Justice Center and the Neighbourhood Justice Centre have been the subject of extensive evaluation, and to positive effect, but evaluation is never a 'once-and-its-done' process.

A good example of the enormity of the task of measurability was with the North Liverpool Community Justice Centre which closed after eight years, in part because of gaps or failures in some of its evaluative assessments.[2] For the Ministry of Justice the cost of operating the Centre could not be supported by its limited caseload.[3] While there were a number of explanations for the Centre's closure – including criticism of the location chosen for the Centre as well as cuts in relevant support services – evaluations had commented negatively on its rates of reduced recidivism and order compliance.[4] One of the key obstacles for the Centre was that there had been suggestions that defendants sentenced at the Centre were more intensively supervised than in mainstream courts.[5] And although there were high rates of approval for its presiding officer, Judge David Fletcher, and of the Centre generally,[6] there were conflicting reports of the Centre's success. While, 76% of respondents in one survey cited that, more than with other court encounters, they had benefited from problem-solving meetings,[7] there were reports of poor rates of a sense of safety in the community[8] and an absence of data showing improvements from the 'community oriented' and 'holistic' nature of the service provided by the Centre.[9]

The North Liverpool experience highlights that for Community Justice Centres there is a need for clear and quantifiable justice data which can be used to benchmark a Centre's progress. This data, particularly comparable control groups, can often be difficult to come by[10] and data, when available, is not necessarily in an easily translatable form. For the Red Hook Community Justice Center, the comparison data that was used was of offenders from the same area who were arrested at weekends and therefore diverted to more mainstream justice avenues.[11] This provided a very useful control group for those who were arrested during the week and had their hearing at the Red Hook Community Justice Center.

Data collection and data expertise needs to also be suitably funded so that information gathering is happening continuously and at the touchpoints where it is most needed. Without this it is very difficult to demonstrate that Community Justice Centres, while being funded to do 'community justice', are meeting key performance indicators that actually work. They need to be able to make a difference while showing tangible evidence to support this. This was a clear gap for the North Liverpool Centre.[12] As one report recounted:

> For all the positivity of Centre staff about innovation and its achievements, there were serious limitations to the Centre being able to evidence the contribution it made to the objectives set for community justice. . . . This is not to say that the Centre isn't achieving significant outcomes, but that it is unable to demonstrate effectiveness.[13]

There is a need for diverse data collection, including in relation to multifaceted aspects such as how the Centre has engaged with the community, the degree to which it has improved local well-being as well as individuals' experience of the court process.[14] As research on how to evaluate data, the Hartford Community Court found this has to include both an assessment of program implementation and its impact while also demonstrating what the situation would have been in the absence of the community court program.[15] It has also been concluded that to track success and areas for improvement, 'open-ended interviews'[16] with participants are vital and can also provide greater depth to evaluation reports.

However, it should not be thought that the work of the Centre is entirely removed from its evaluation. Working closely with defendants, community members and advisory groups can provide valuable and often informal feedback on what needs to be tweaked in a Centre's operations, often well before a final evaluation is published. It can also help sell the value of the Centre.[17] Procedural justice theory supports the notion that the nature of community interaction will influence the legitimacy and acceptance of a Centre in the community.[18] As Fagan explains:

> It can build legitimacy because of the accretion of positive experiences of individuals who go through the court and who use the building. . . . [T]his is communicated to the community at large through both the direct experience of the citizens in the court and also by some vicarious knowledge that they get because their neighbors are having contact with the court and going through the court. . . . All of these mechanisms are pathways to legitimacy.[19]

A further challenge is being able to pinpoint the exact source of any improvement in justice outcomes. How much of a lowering in a community's crime rate stems from an increased police presence, greater employment opportunities or urban renewal? If a Community Justice Centre is positively evaluated, how much of its success can be attributed to its activities and how much to external factors? How is credit to be fairly attributed when the variables are complex and intersecting? As Ross determines:

> like the Red Hook evaluation, one is left with the conclusion that the observed changes in crime rates are what would be desired from an effective community court in Yarra, without being able to say definitively that they are directly caused by the activities at the NJC [Neighbourhood Justice Centre].[20]

What is evident is that it is not possible to assess Community Justice Centres solely in terms of rates of recidivism and observance of court orders.[21] Instead, richer mixed-data evaluations are needed to report on a variety of varying factors such as community trust, safety, levels of community embeddedness and the defendants' experiences of the Centre.[22] But as Berman states, part of the role of Community Justice Centres must be to 'chang[e] the questions asked of the justice system'[23] and for their evaluations to do the same.[24] This is a logical extension of the holistic approach which rests at the heart of the Community Justice model. As Community Justice Centres seek to operate differently, and to meet goals not envisioned or achievable in standard courts, it cannot be assumed that they can be evaluated in identical ways. It is inevitable that there will be stark differences in evaluation design even between Community Justice Centres, while all will require ongoing funding for this important purpose. As Halsey and de Vel-Palumbo recognise, 'There is a need to be permanently reflexive about the therapeutic space such that measurement and evaluation – understanding how and why things work or do not work – become key to ongoing success'.[25]

Boundaries

Overreach

Problem-solving courts generally, of which Community Justice Centres form one example, can be prone to criticism of overreach into citizens' lives. In seeking to tackle some of the underlying issues bringing an individual consistently into contact with the criminal justice system, it can be unclear where the role of the court starts and ends. Ultimately, is the provision of services at the courthouse door what the justice system is designed for?[26] It also has to be considered whether, through this justice 'overreach', communities may start to expect more out of the justice system than most mainstream courts are ever going to be able to provide.[27] If so, will this eat into the confidence the public place in the justice system as a whole?[28]

On a more individual level, the legalisation of service delivery can change the authenticity of participant engagement. There can also be questions as to whether that engagement is always chosen or completely voluntary and whether it is overshadowed by 'paternalism'.[29] This is magnified by the sense that a defendant working through their issues with the support of the Community Justice Centre may have somewhat of a Hobson's choice when the raw alternative can be a mainstream court process.

There are a number of responses to these concerns. First, it is often the case that Community Justice Centres as 'community centres' often provide services to community members and not only those that come before the courts. It is for this reason they are often described as a Centre that contains a court rather than the other way around. Second, if the problem is that social services are being combined with curial ones, Chief Justice Kaye has responded that we have to accept that the traditional ways of operating are just not working:

> That there may be issues, moreover, is not a condemnation of the problem-solving idea, but rather a signal, or reminder, of the need for care in the planning and operation of these courts.[30]

Monitoring and closely evaluating defendants' experiences is crucial here but also ensuring that interventions are appropriately targeted and collaboratively crafted. There is also a need to experiment with different ways of engaging defendants. Berman and Feinblatt note that some solution-focused models enable defendants to 'test out treatment while their case is pending' and can then be in a better position to make a decision about what course they want to choose.[31] It also needs to be recognised that mainstream justice models can trample on individual agency through a range of direct and indirect pressures.

The related concern though is whether the problems in peoples' lives can be better overcome by addressing systemic failings rather than curial entry-points.[32] With this innovation we are seeing a change in the role played by the criminal justice system. It is not being expected to make everything better. One evaluation of the Neighbourhood Justice Centre observed that:

> dealing with crime under a community justice model means that the justice arm of the state should help build community resilience, in

relation not only to crime, but to other types of problems which make crime possible or more likely. In this latter sense, community justice recognises that minor social disputes of a non-criminal nature, or instances of neighbourhood and social neglect, can be precursors to or markers of crime.[33]

The system's role is being 'realign[ed]' while recognising that 'it's not the primary producer of public safety and community well-being'.[34]

In the United States it has been argued that offences that are commonly brought before some Community Justice Centres are not ones that should come to the courts in the first place.[35] Quality-of-life crimes such as turnstile jumping or public urination have other means of address whether that be by fine or dismissal and can be seen as paternalistically elongating an individual's involvement with the justice system.[36] Berman and Feinblatt have argued in response that the model ensures that offences receive a calibrated consequence and that failing to do this can 'send the wrong message to offenders, victims, police, and community residents'.[37] In response to criticism of the Tenderloin Community Justice Center it was said that:

> proponents point out that the benefits of using the courts to promote positive changes in the lives of offenders and their communities far outweigh any perceived paternalism, and that the therapeutic approach is no more coercive than more traditional models of adjudication.[38]

Creating community?

Malkin has raised a different concern and that is the degree to which the institution of a Community Justice Centre needs a 'community' to engage with and accordingly can 'fabricat[e]' one where it might not otherwise exist in the same form.[39] She explains that 'the community becomes an imagined group served by the court' and 'becomes the objects as opposed to the subject of the actions taking place in its name'.[40] Malkin is right that there is a risk that a community can become idealised[41] or its needs homogenised; but that is less a criticism of the Community Justice Centre model *per se* but about the need for thorough neighbourhood consultation on a level playing field, centre co-creation and the importance of an ongoing community dialogue.[42] There is also a need to ensure that the reach of the Centre engages with the neighbourhood as a whole, including individuals or groups who are potentially marginalised by traditional conceptions or activities of the local community and that some sectors do not dominate the community conversation.[43] For instance efforts to engage with the community in setting up the Tenderloin Community Justice Center described the Center as:

> the product of the community from the beginning of the planning process. The steering committee is made up of government officers and community members. Planners engaged in a lengthy survey of the neighborhoods that will be served by the CJC, including an extensive effort to survey homeless persons and indigent residents of the Tenderloin and South of Market areas. The survey provided planners with insight into what residents want from the court, what they like about the current state of law enforcement and what they feel are failures of the status quo. As the CJC continues to operate, input from the community will be regularly incorporated into the growth and development of the project, ensuring that the court is truly a product of the community.[44]

It is also vital that Centres do not see communities as there to serve the Centre instrumentally[45] and drive its success but rather as the Centre serving the community (or communities) of which it forms a part. For this to genuinely work, there is a need for governance structures which 'empower the community'.[46] Co-creation and governance must take particularly precedence with First Nations communities and the need to ensure that the diversity of community interests are respected and that leadership roles are assigned to Elders and community-controlled groups.[47] As Malkin explains, what is needed is a 'clear mechanism in place that prioritizes how and why these courts are there for the community'.[48] This also requires centres to change along with the community. For example, the Neighbourhood Justice Centre is actively working with the fact that more and more of crimes committed in the City of Yarra are committed by non-Yarra residents.[49]

Relatedly, there can be a risk that the community comes to lean on the Centre to too great a degree. Lanni discusses how what can emerge is that the 'role of the judge and expert social service personnel' reduce the voice of the community and the approaches it pursues.[50] Ultimately, the community needs to work with but not 'be' the Centre or be solely defined by it.[51] This is especially evident when the time comes for a changeover in the judicial officer. Community Justice Centres need to ensure that the Centre's identity and community connection is not too caught up in the persona of a particular judicial officer.[52]

Specialised knowledge

For judicial officers there is a clear need for specialised training.[53] If the court is to work with a defendant to identify the underlying issues fuelling their offending, there needs to be a recognition of the importance of a broad range of skill sets[54] as well as the complexity of identifying the root problems in the first place.[55] The Harlem Community Justice Center, for instance, has adopted an 'evidence-based screening tool' to ensure that service provision is tailored to an individual's needs.[56] At the Neighbourhood Justice Centre, the enabling Act requires the appointment of the Centre's Magistrate to be done with reference to the 'Magistrate's knowledge of, or experience in the application of, the principles of therapeutic jurisprudence and restorative justice'.[57] And, in fact, the Magistrate who has been the judicial officer at the Neighbourhood Justice Centre, Magistrate David Fanning, is trained in both social work and law.

Fairness

Questions also arise as to whether defendants in the Community Justice Centre context may have their legal rights affected or the independence and impartiality of the bench compromised by the integrated 'team' approach, the less-adversarial operation of the court and even community connections.[58] Community Justice Centres cannot ignore these concerns and need to put in place mechanisms to counter accusations of unfairness and continually evaluate defendants' experiences. The model needs to ensure that defendant rights are not sacrificed to open up access to available services and alternative sentencing options. But at the same time it should not be assumed that 'less adversarial' means that a defendant lacks proper or 'zealous' representation or a chance to challenge the case against them.[59] At the Neighbourhood Justice Centre for instance, to keep the requisite protections in place, the Magistrate is not involved in problem-solving meetings. All communications with the Magistrate occur in open court with the defendant present.[60]

There can be concerns associated with the power assigned to the judicial officer who can come to traverse both the court and community spheres as well as liaising with key stakeholders.[61] Centres usually establish processes to carefully manage this. At the Midtown Community Court there is a clear division of responsibility whereby the judge, although joining advisory board sessions, avoids 'manag[ing] community relations', with this the responsibility of other staff.[62] Feinblatt and Berman recognise that:

> judges must struggle to identify which forms of interaction with community residents are acceptable and which are not – and clearly communicate their expectations to the local community. They must also think hard about what types of information regarding community

problems or concerns should be taken into consideration in deciding individual cases.[63]

Judge Calabrese has stated that community knowledge is pivotal to being 'effective' and that there is no need 'to be completely blind to community issues to be fair'.[64] It is also the case that should a potential conflict arise a court matter can always be transferred.[65]

Obstacles

The obstacles faced by the Community Justice Centre model inevitably vary as much as the Centres themselves. This variability represents an obstacle in itself. For instance, Nolan has raised how countries adopting problem-solving models, including Community Justice Centres, must carefully appraise how the model sits with their different legal and cultural settings.[66] The bespoke nature of Community Justice Centres mean that what works in one area or region may not work in another, even within the same jurisdiction. Further, some sectors of a community may not be adequately served or suitably buy in to the innovation, or they may seek to engage with the Centre in quite different ways.

One of the key obstacles is the financial outlay associated with the consultation, design and implementation of a Community Justice Centre, particularly if this is likely to involve a new building or significant refurbishment. There is also the need to convince government stakeholders that their success does not only derive from an inflated budget or from reductions elsewhere. Criticisms of one San Francisco pilot concentrated on the cost of a new Centre and the potential impact on service delivery in the community if this 'would require cutting the very services the CJC would help provide'.[67] Experiences such as the Neighbourhood Justice Centre have shown that there can be cost efficiencies associated with service co-location. Additional examples show that spending justice money upfront can avoid an increased outlay down the track when recidivism and order compliance are able to be addressed by a justice reform.[68] Centres don't have to be expensive. New premises are not necessarily required, with the pivotal consideration being whether the location and venue chosen has community buy-in and support.[69]

Another common obstacle is overcoming perceptions that community justice is a justice-light option. Magistrate David Fanning has challenged this in the context of the Neighbourhood Justice Centre explaining 'it's not a soft option, and it's not an option that excludes imprisonment in appropriate cases'.[70] This is because for an individual or family to actively work to address complex personal circumstances is often an arduous route to take. It also is not necessarily the case that more serious sentences are precluded in

Community Courts.[71] Interestingly, research with the Vancouver Downtown Community Court found that while some of those surveyed perceived it as a weak justice avenue, others felt it was too tough on defendants.[72] As Berman and Feinblatt explain, 'these courts send a double message: all offenders must be held accountable for their crime, no matter how small; a court can use its coercive power to move offenders towards rehabilitation'.[73] This approach is something that can engender a considerable degree of community traction.[74] As Judge Calabrese has commented:

> What I've found – and I was surprised at this – is that when you ask the community what they want, they want defendants to be given an opportunity to use services, even people with longtime records. I thought that would be a little bit of a problem to convince people in Red Hook before the court opened, but right away they were saying, "let's give them a chance."[75]

An associated issue is the degree to which Community Justice Centre models are too limited in their operation both in a jurisdictional and place-based sense. The budget and workload of larger mainstream courts often leave no resources for smaller site-based justice solutions. In the study of the Vancouver Downtown Community Court, one interviewee said that, 'it would be helpful if DCC [Downtown Community Court] was a full service court that was able to do trials as well as guilty pleas. Until that occurs, DCC will always be considered a court "soft on crime"'.[76] As discussed in Chapter 5, Washington DC trialled a centralised Community Justice Centre model that was run through the central law court but had local reach. What is evident is that the boundaries of the Community Justice Centre model are not definitive and can be tailored to the needs of a particular community or communities.[77] For example, the Neighbourhood Justice Centre in the City of Yarra was chosen for a range of reasons, including its high crime rate which was second only to Melbourne and while not running contested trials, hears a broad range of offences.[78] Similarly, the Kenora Bi-Cultural Community Justice Centre in Ontario is being designed to widen its reach through the use of a centre network.[79] The potential of a mobile 'hybrid' model has also been recommended in the context of remote Western Australia, showcasing the potential diversity and efficiencies of the model.[80]

The experience of the Brownsville Community Justice Center discussed in Chapter 3 highlighted that a key perceived limitation with the instigation of a Community Justice Centre is whether it would bring about a fundamental change to the nature of the local area. Locals were concerned that the Center would mean that Brownsville would change in a way that would mean it no longer belonged to the local community. A parallel fear that can emerge is of community displacement.[81] In Brownsville, the approach was to work with the neighbourhood to co-create each aspect of the Centre and its activities to ensure that the community was empowered by and had ownership of the Centre, such as through its Belmont Revitalization Project.[82]

Conclusion

Any justice innovation requires careful analysis and sustained evaluation. Community Justice Centres demonstrate the need for this to be done with a full appreciation of the uniqueness of the innovation and avoidance of cookie-cutter justice evaluation tools. Community Justice Centres fundamentally change the role of the court and its relationship with the community. This means that evaluations of their success need to be calibrated to take account of this. It also means that their institution, implementation and operation needs to be undertaken with a distinct awareness of the new terrain the justice innovation is entering and with an authentic partnership with and 'leadership'[83] by the community which the Centre is designed to serve. This leadership means that Community Justice Centres can work with local communities to design Centres that belong to them and which have the requisite knowledge and buy-in to be able to work through with the community any concerns that the Centre may present.

Notes

1 See, e.g. Rachel Swaner, 'Community Courts' in Gerben Bruinsma and David Weisburd (eds), *Encyclopedia of Criminology and Criminal Justice* (Springer, 2014) 414; Greg Berman, *Principles of Community Justice: A Guide for Community Court Planners* (Bureau of Justice Assistance, 2010) 12, http://assets. justice.vic.gov.au/njc/resources/9a637e19-fdc2-45b3-9349-34ae5e37e08f/03.+ principals+of+community+justice.pdf

2 For a detailed study of this see: Sarah Murray and Harry Blagg, 'Reconceptualising Community Justice Centre Evaluations – Lessons from the North Liverpool Experience' (2018) 27(2) *Griffith Law Review* 254–69. There were other challenges for the Centre as well, such as doubts surrounding the site chosen for the Centre and the community consultation process which accompanied it.

3 BBC, 'Community Justice Centre in Liverpool to Be Closed', 23 October 2013, www.bbc.com/news/uk-england-merseyside-24638951. See also George Mair and Matthew Millings, *Doing Justice Locally: The North Liverpool Community Justice Centre* (Centre for Crime and Justice Studies, 2011) 10, https://assets. justice.vic.gov.au/njc/resources/488e89e5-f5ac-4c73-a4e6-e32236e1bb1c/ doing_justice_locally_northliverpool.pdf

4 Lucy Booth, Adam Altoft, Rachel Dubourg, Miguel Gonçalves and Catriona Mirrlees-Black, *North Liverpool Community Justice Centre: Analysis of Re-Offending Rates and Efficiency of Court Processes* (Ministry of Justice Research

Series 10/12, 2012); Katharine McKenna, *Evaluation of the North Liverpool Community Justice Centre* (Ministry of Justice Research Series 12/7, 2007). For a detailed discussion of some of the reasons for its closure see: Murray and Blagg, 'Reconceptualising Community Justice Centre Evaluations', above n 2.

5 Booth et al., *North Liverpool Community Justice Centre*, above n 4; Darrick Jolliffe and David Farrington, *Initial Evaluation of Reconviction Rates in Community Justice Initiatives* (Ministry of Justice Research Summary 9/9, 2009) 4, www.crim.cam.ac.uk/people/academic_research/david_farrington/commjmoj. pdf

6 S. Llewellyn-Thomas and G. Prior, *North Liverpool Community Justice Centre: Surveys of Local Residents* (Ministry of Justice Research Series 13/7, 2007) III; McKenna, *Evaluation of the North Liverpool Community Justice Centre*, above n 4, VI.

7 McKenna, *Evaluation of the North Liverpool Community Justice Centre*, above n 4, 28.

8 Llewellyn-Thomas and Prior, *North Liverpool Community Justice Centre*, above n 6.

9 Mair and Millings, *Doing Justice Locally*, above n 3, 5.

10 Cynthia Lee et al., *A Community Court Grows in Brooklyn: A Comprehensive Evaluation of the Red Hook Community Justice Center* (National Centre for State Courts, 2013) 12; Stuart Ross, 'Evaluating Neighbourhood Justice: Measuring and Attributing Outcomes for a Community Justice Program' (2015) November 499 *Trends & Issues in Crime and Criminal Justice* 3, www.aic.gov. au/media_library/publications/tandi_pdf/tandi499.pdf

11 Lee et al., *A Community Court Grows in Brooklyn*, above n 10, 15.

12 Mair and Millings, *Doing Justice Locally*, above n 3, 5.

13 Ibid.

14 John S. Goldkamp et al., *Developing an Evaluation Plan for Community Courts-Assessing the Hartford Community Court Model* (Bureau of Justice Assistance, 2001) 30–2.

15 Ibid. 39.

16 Susan Flynn, 'The Red Hook Community Justice Center: An Evaluation of a Community Court' (2005) 33 *Journal of Psychiatry & Law* 43, 98.

17 David R. Karp and Todd R. Clear, 'Community Justice: A Conceptual Framework' (2000) 2 *Criminal Justice* 323, 350.

18 Sarah Murray, 'Keeping It in the Neighbourhood? Neighbourhood Courts in the Australian Context' (2009) 35(1) *Monash University Law Review* 74, 87.

19 Michael Rempel et al., 'What Works and What Does Not – Symposium' (2002) 29 *Fordham Urban Law Journal* 1929, 1939–40 (Jeffrey Fagan).

20 Ross, 'Evaluating Neighbourhood Justice', above n 10, 3.

21 Ibid. 7; Victoria Malkin, 'Community Courts and the Process of Accountability: Consensus and Conflict at the Red Hook Community Justice Center' (2003) 40(4) *American Criminal Law Review* 1573, 1576, 1585.

22 See, e.g. Diana Karafin, 'Community Courts Across the Globe: A Survey of Goals, Performance Measures and Operations', 2008, 22–3, www. courtinnovation.org/sites/default/files/community_court_world.pdf

23 Berman, *Principles of Community Justice: A Guide for Community Court Planners*, above n 1, 10.

24 Ross, 'Evaluating Neighbourhood Justice', above n 10, 7.

25 Mark Halsey and Melissa de Vel-Palumbo, 'Courts as Empathic Spaces: Reflections on the Neighbourhood Justice Centre' (2018) 27(2) *Griffith Law Review* 182, 198.
26 Victoria Malkin, 'Problem-Solving in Community Courts: Who Decides the Problem?' in Paul Higgins and Mitchell B. Mackinem (eds), *Problem-Solving Courts: Justice for the Twenty-First Century?* (Praeger, 2009) 139, 155; Richard C. Boldt, 'A Circumspect Look at Problem-Solving Courts' in Paul Higgins and Mitchell B. Mackinem (eds), *Problem-Solving Courts: Justice for the Twenty-First Century?* (Praeger, 2009) 3, 18; Robin Steinberg and Skyla Albertson, 'Broken Windows Policing and Community Courts: An Unholy Alliance' (2016) 37 *Cardozo Law Review* 995, 1015; Michael Cobden and Ron Albers, 'Beyond the Squabble: Putting the Tenderloin Community Justice Center in Context' (2010) 7 *Hastings Race & Poverty Law Journal* 53, 61.
27 Greg Berman and Aubrey Fox, 'From the Margins to the Mainstream: Community Justice at the Crossroads' (2001) 22(2) *Justice System Journal* 189, 204 (Bill Ritter).
28 Murray, 'Keeping It in the Neighbourhood', above n 18, 94.
29 Greg Berman, 'What Is a Traditional Judge Anyway? Problem Solving in the State Courts' (2000) 84(2) *Judicature* 78, 85.
30 Judith S. Kaye, 'Delivering Justice Today: A Problem-Solving Approach' (2004) 22 *Yale Law & Policy Review* 148–9.
31 Greg Berman and John Feinblatt, *Good Courts – The Case for Problem-Solving Justice* (New York Press, 2005) 179.
32 Berman and Fox, 'From the Margins to the Mainstream', above n 27, 203 (Brad Lander); Anthony Thompson, 'Courting Disorder: Some Thoughts on Community Courts' (2002) 10 *Washington University Journal of Law and Policy* 63, 90.
33 M. Halsey et al. quoted in Neighbourhood Justice Centre, 'Strategic Plan 2019–2023', 2019, 9, www.neighbourhoodjustice.vic.gov.au/sites/default/files/embridge_cache/emshare/original/public/2020/04/21/3a7da1bdf/NJC%20Strat%20Plan%202019-2023.pdf
34 Berman and Fox, 'From the Margins to the Mainstream', above n 27, 200 (Walter Dickey).
35 Thompson, 'Courting Disorder', above n 32, 82.
36 Steinberg and Albertson, 'Broken Windows Policing and Community Courts', above n 26, 1012, 1016.
37 Berman and Feinblatt, *Good Courts*, above n 31, 175.
38 Cobden and Albers, 'Beyond the Squabble', above n 26, 55.
39 Malkin, 'Problem-Solving in Community Courts: Who Decides the Problem?', above n 26, 143. See also Nikolas Rose, 'The Death of the Social? Re-figuring the Territory of Government' (1996) 25(3) *Economy & Society* 327, 331–3.
40 Ibid. See also Steinberg and Albertson, 'Broken Windows Policing and Community Courts', above n 26, 1019; Berman and Fox, 'From the Margins to the Mainstream', above n 27, 202 (Eric Lane); Jeffrey Fagan and Victoria Malkin, 'Theorizing Community Justice Through Community Courts' (2003) 30 *Fordham Urban Law Journal* 897, 950.
41 Barbara Yngvesson, 'Local People, Local Problems, and Neighborhood Justice: The Discourse of "Community" in San Francisco Community Boards' in Sally Engle Merry and Neal Milner (eds), *The Possibility of Popular Justice: A Case Study of Community Mediation in the United States* (University of Michigan Press, 1993) 382.

42 Accordingly, McCoy has identified the need for 'caution' before rushing to implement new problem-solving initiatives: Candace McCoy, 'The Politics of Problem-Solving: An Overview of the Origins and Development of Therapeutic Courts' (2003) 40 *American Criminal Law Review* 1513.

43 Murray, 'Keeping It in the Neighbourhood', above n 18, 93.

44 Cobden and Albers, 'Beyond the Squabble', above n 26, 60.

45 Malkin, 'Problem-Solving in Community Courts: Who Decides the Problem?', above n 26, 145.

46 Victoria Malkin, 'Community Courts and the Process of Accountability: Consensus and Conflict at the Red Hook Community Justice Center' (2003) 40(4) *American Criminal Law Review* 1573. See also Todd W. Daloz, 'Challenges of Tough Love: Examining San Francisco's Community Justice Center and Evaluating Its Prospects for Success' (2008) 6 *Hastings Race & Poverty Law Journal* 55, 85.

47 Sarah Murray, Harry Blagg and Suzie May, 'Doing Justice Differently: A Community Justice Centre for Western Australia: A Feasibility Study Final Report', 2018, 29–30, www.law.uwa.edu.au/__data/assets/pdf_file/0011/3151757/FEASIBILITY-STUDY-REPORT.pdf

48 Malkin, 'Problem-Solving in Community Courts: Who Decides the Problem?', above n 26, 155.

49 Neighbourhood Justice Centre, 'Strategic Plan 2019–2023', above n 33, 14.

50 Adriaan Lanni, 'The Future of Community Justice' (2004) 40 *Harvard Civil Rights – Civil Liberties Law Review* 359, 382.

51 Malkin, 'Problem-Solving in Community Courts: Who Decides the Problem?' above n 26, 152–3.

52 Murray, 'Keeping It in the Neighbourhood?', above n 18, 92.

53 Arie Freiberg, 'Problem-Oriented Courts: Innovative Solutions to Intractable Problems?' (2001) 11 *Journal of Judicial Administration* 8, 23; Thompson, 'Courting Disorder', above n 32, 93.

54 Swaner, 'Community Courts', above n 1, 414, 415; Ibid.

55 Freiberg, 'Problem-Oriented Courts', above n 53, 22.

56 Berman, *Principles of Community Justice: A Guide for Community Court Planners*, above n 1, 7.

57 *Magistrates' Court Act 1989* (Vic), s 4M(5)(a).

58 See, e.g. Adriaan Lanni, 'The Future of Community Justice' (2005) 40(2) *Harvard Civil Rights-Civil Liberties Law Review* 359, 385; Freiberg, 'Problem-Oriented Courts', above n 53, 23; Thompson, 'Courting Disorder', above n 32, 93–4; Daloz, 'Challenges of Tough Love', above n 46, 81–2; Gal and Hadar Dancig-Rosenberg, 'I Am Starting to Believe in the Word "Justice": Lessons from an Ethnographic Study on Community Courts' (2020) 68 *American Journal of Comparative Law* 376, 384. For a study on the constitutionality of less-adversarial processes in the Australian state context see: Sarah Murray, *The Remaking of the Courts- Less-Adversarial Practice and the Constitutional Role of the Judiciary in Australia* (Federation Press, 2014) chapter 6.

59 John Feinblatt and Greg Berman, 'Community Courts: A Brief Primer' (2001) January *United States Attorneys' Bulletin* 33, 37; Berman and Feinblatt, *Good Courts*, above n 31, 187; Alex Calabrese, 'The Impact of Problem Solving Courts on the Lawyer's Role and Ethics' (2002) 29 *Fordham Urban Law Journal* 1892, 1916; Greg Berman and Aubrey Fox, 'From the Benches and Trenches – Justice in Red Hook' (2005) 26(1) *Justice System Journal* 77, 86.

60   Murray et al., 'Doing Justice Differently', above n 47, 17.
61   Daloz, 'Challenges of Tough Love', above n 46, 82.
62   Feinblatt and Berman, 'Community Courts: A Brief Primer', above n 59, 36.
63   Ibid.
64   Berman and Feinblatt, *Good Courts*, above n 31, 187.
65   Ibid. 186.
66   James L. Nolan, *Legal Accents, Legal Borrowing: The International Problem-Solving Court Movement* (Princeton University Press, 2009) 14.
67   Cobden and Albers, 'Beyond the Squabble', above n 26, 61.
68   Greg Berman and Aubrey Fox, 'The Future of Problem-Solving Justice: An International Perspective' (2010) 10 *University of Maryland Law & Justice Race, Religion, Gender & Class* 1, 11.
69   Murray et al., 'Doing Justice Differently', above n 47, 32, 39–40.
70   Anita Barraud, 'One-Stop Legal Shop', *The Law Report – ABC Radio National*, 3 April 2007, www.abc.net.au/radionational/programs/lawreport/one-stop-legal-shop/3400580
71   Feinblatt and Berman, 'Community Courts: A Brief Primer', above n 59, 37.
72   Margaret Jackson et al., 'Compilation of Research on the Vancouver Downtown Community Court 2008 to 2012', 2012, 95, https://www2.gov.bc.ca/assets/gov/law-crime-and-justice/courthouse-services/community-court/dcc-research-compilation.pdf
73   Feinblatt and Berman, 'Community Courts: A Brief Primer', above n 59, 37.
74   Ibid.
75   Berman and Fox, 'From the Margins to the Mainstream', above n 27, 198.
76   Jackson et al., 'Compilation of Research on the Vancouver Downtown Community Court 2008 to 2012', above n 72, 68.
77   Gregory Toomey, 'Community Courts 101: A Quick Survey Course' (2006) 42(2) *Idaho Law Review* 383, 408.
78   Ross, 'Evaluating Neighbourhood Justice', above n 10, 3.
79   Ministry of the Attorney-General, 'Community Justice Centres', 2018, https://hsjcc.on.ca/wp-content/uploads/NY-HSJCC-Community-Justice-Centres.pdf
80   Sarah Murray, Tamara Tulich and Harry Blagg, 'The Innovative Magistrate and Legitimacy: Lessons for a Mobile "Solution-Focused" Model' (2017) 40(2) *University of New South Wales Law Journal* 897.
81   Toomey, 'Community Courts 101', above n 77, 408; Daloz, 'Challenges of Tough Love', above n 46, 85.
82   Center for Court Innovation, 'The Belmont Revitalization Project: Reimagining an Avenue', 2015, www.courtinnovation.org/articles/belmont-revitalization-project-reimagining-avenue?%3Bmode=project&%3Bproject=Brownsville%20Community%20Justice%20Center&url=project/brownsville-community-justice-center
83   Berman and Fox, 'From the Margins to the Mainstream', above n 27, 197 (Peggy McGarry).

Bibliography

Journals, reports, books, media and papers

Barraud, Anita. 'One-Stop Legal Shop', 3 April 2007, www.abc.net.au/radio national/programs/lawreport/one-stop-legal-shop/3400580

BBC. 'Community Justice Centre in Liverpool to Be Closed', 23 October 2013, www.bbc.com/news/uk-england-merseyside-24638951.

Berman, Greg. *Principles of Community Justice: A Guide for Community Court Planners* (Bureau of Justice Assistance, 2010), http://assets.justice.vic.gov.au/njc/resources/9a637e19-fdc2-45b3-9349-34ae5e37e08f/03.+principals+of+community+justice.pdf

Berman, Greg. 'What Is a Traditional Judge Anyway? Problem Solving in the State Courts' (2000) 84(2) *Judicature* 78.

Berman, Greg and John Feinblatt. *Good Courts – The Case for Problem-Solving Justice* (New York Press, 2005).

Berman, Greg and Aubrey Fox. 'From the Benches and Trenches – Justice in Red Hook' (2005) 26(1) *The Justice System Journal* 77.

Berman, Greg and Aubrey Fox. 'From the Margins to the Mainstream: Community Justice at the Crossroads' (2001) 22(2) *Justice System Journal* 189.

Berman, Greg and Aubrey Fox. 'The Future of Problem-Solving Justice: An International Perspective' (2010) 10 *University of Maryland Law & Justice Race, Religion, Gender & Class* 1.

Booth, Lucy et al. *North Liverpool Community Justice Centre: Analysis of Re-Offending Rates and Efficiency of Court Processes* (Ministry of Justice Research Series 10/12, 2012).

Calabrese, Alex. 'The Impact of Problem Solving Courts on the Lawyer's Role and Ethics' (2002) 29 *Fordham Urban Law Journal* 1892.

Center for Court Innovation. 'The Belmont Revitalization Project: Reimagining an Avenue', 2015, www.courtinnovation.org/articles/belmont-revitalization-project-reimagining-avenue?%3Bmode=project&%3Bproject=Brownsville%20Community%20Justice%20Center&url=project/brownsville-community-justice-center

Cobden, Michael and Judge Ron Albers. 'Beyond the Squabble: Putting the Tenderloin Community Justice Center in Context' (2010) 7 *Hastings Race & Poverty Law Journal* 53.

Daloz, Todd W. 'Challenges of Tough Love: Examining San Francisco's Community Justice Center and Evaluating Its Prospects for Success' (2008) 6 *Hastings Race & Poverty Law Journal* 55.

Fagan, Jeffrey and Victoria Malkin. 'Theorizing Community Justice Through Community Courts' (2003) 30 *Fordham Urban Law Journal* 897.

Feinblatt, John and Greg Berman. 'Community Courts: A Brief Primer' (2001) January *United States Attorneys' Bulletin* 33.

Flynn, Susan. 'The Red Hook Community Justice Center: An Evaluation of a Community Court' (2005) 33 *Journal of Psychiatry & Law* 43.

Freiberg, Arie. 'Problem-Oriented Courts: Innovative Solutions to Intractable Problems?' (2001) 11 *Journal of Judicial Administration* 8.

Gal, Tali and Hadar Dancig-Rosenberg. 'I Am Starting to Believe in the Word "Justice": Lessons from an Ethnographic Study on Community Courts' (2020) 68 *American Journal of Comparative Law* 376.

Goldkamp, John S. et al. *Developing an Evaluation Plan for Community Courts–Assessing the Hartford Community Court Model* (Bureau of Justice Assistance, 2001).

Halsey, Mark and Melissa de Vel-Palumbo. 'Courts as Empathic Spaces: Reflections on the Neighbourhood Justice Centre' (2018) 27(2) *Griffith Law Review* 182.

Higgins, Paul and Mitchell B. Mackinem (eds). *Problem-Solving Courts: Justice for the Twenty-First Century?* (Praeger, 2009).

Jackson, Margaret et al. 'Compilation of Research on the Vancouver Downtown Community Court 2008 to 2012', 2012, https://www2.gov.bc.ca/assets/gov/law-crime-and-justice/courthouse-services/community-court/dcc-research-compilation.pdf

Jolliffe, Darrick and David Farrington. *Initial Evaluation of Reconviction Rates in Community Justice Initiatives* (Ministry of Justice Research Summary 9/9, 2009), www.crim.cam.ac.uk/people/academic_research/david_farrington/commjmoj.pdf

Karafin, Diana. 'Community Courts Across the Globe: A Survey of Goals, Performance Measures and Operations', 2008, www.courtinnovation.org/sites/default/files/community_court_world.pdf

Karp, David R. and Todd R. Clear. 'Community Justice: A Conceptual Framework' (2000) 2 *Criminal Justice* 323.

Kaye, Judith S. 'Delivering Justice Today: A Problem-Solving Approach' (2004) 22 *Yale Law & Policy Review* 125.

Laani, Adriaan. 'The Future of Community Justice' (2004) 40 *Harvard Civil Rights – Civil Liberties Law Review* 359.

Lee, Cynthia et al. *A Community Court Grows in Brooklyn: A Comprehensive Evaluation of the Red Hook Community Justice Center* (National Centre for State Courts, 2013).

Llewellyn-Thomas, S. and G. Prior. *North Liverpool Community Justice Centre: Surveys of Local Residents* (Ministry of Justice Research Series 13/7, 2007).

Mair, George and Matthew Millings. *Doing Justice Locally: The North Liverpool Community Justice Centre* (Centre for Crime and Justice Studies, 2011), https://assets.justice.vic.gov.au/njc/resources/488e89e5-f5ac-4c73-a4e6-e32236e1bb1c/doing_justice_locally_northliverpool.pdf

Malkin, Victoria. 'Community Courts and the Process of Accountability: Consensus and Conflict at the Red Hook Community Justice Center' (2003) 40(4) *American Criminal Law Review* 1573.

McCoy, Candace. 'The Politics of Problem-Solving: An Overview of the Origins and Development of Therapeutic Courts' (2003) 40 *American Criminal Law Review* 1513.

McKenna, Katharine. *Evaluation of the North Liverpool Community Justice Centre* (Ministry of Justice Research Series 12/7, 2007).

Merry, Sally Engle and Neal Milner (eds). *The Possibility of Popular Justice: A Case Study of Community Mediation in the United States* (University of Michigan Press, 1993).

Ministry of the Attorney-General. 'Community Justice Centres', 2018, https://hsjcc.on.ca/wp-content/uploads/NY-HSJCC-Community-Justice-Centres.pdf

Murray, Sarah. 'Keeping It in the Neighbourhood? Neighbourhood Courts in the Australian Context' (2009) 35(1) *Monash University Law Review* 74.

Murray, Sarah. *The Remaking of the Courts- Less-Adversarial Practice and the Constitutional Role of the Judiciary in Australia* (Federation Press, 2014).

Murray, Sarah and Harry Blagg. 'Reconceptualising Community Justice Centre Evaluations – Lessons from the North Liverpool Experience' (2018) 27(2) *Griffith Law Review* 254.

Murray, Sarah, Harry Blagg and Suzie May. 'Doing Justice Differently: A Community Justice Centre for Western Australia: A Feasibility Study Final Report', 2018, 29–30, www.law.uwa.edu.au/__data/assets/pdf_file/0011/3151757/FEASIBILITY-STUDY-REPORT.pdf

Murray, Sarah, Tamara Tulich and Harry Blagg. 'The Innovative Magistrate and Legitimacy: Lessons for a Mobile "Solution-Focused" Model' (2017) 40(2) *University of New South Wales Law Journal* 897.

Neighbourhood Justice Centre. 'Strategic Plan 2019–2023', 2019, www.neighbourhoodjustice.vic.gov.au/sites/default/files/embridge_cache/emshare/original/public/2020/04/21/3a7da1bdf/NJC%20Strat%20Plan%202019-2023.pdf

Nolan, James L. *Legal Accents, Legal Borrowing: The International Problem-Solving Court Movement* (Princeton University Press, 2009).

Rempel, Michael et al. 'What Works and What Does Not – Symposium' (2002) 29 *Fordham Urban Law Journal* 1929.

Rose, Nikolas. 'The Death of the Social? Re-figuring the Territory of Government' (1996) 25(3) *Economy & Society* 327.

Ross, Stuart. 'Evaluating Neighbourhood Justice: Measuring and Attributing Outcomes for a Community Justice Program' (2015) November 499 *Trends & Issues in Crime and Criminal Justice*, www.aic.gov.au/media_library/publications/tandi_pdf/tandi499.pdf

Steinberg, Robin and Skyla Albertson. 'Broken Windows Policing and Community Courts: An Unholy Alliance' (2016) 37 *Cardozo Law Review* 995.

Swaner, Rachel. 'Community Courts' in Gerben Bruinsma and David Weisburd (eds), *Encyclopedia of Criminology and Criminal Justice* (Springer, 2014), 414.

Thompson, Anthony. 'Courting Disorder: Some Thoughts on Community Courts' (2002) 10 *Washington University Journal of Law and Policy* 63.

Toomey, Gregory. 'Community Courts 101: A Quick Survey Course' (2006) 42(2) *Idaho Law Review* 383.

Legislation

Magistrates' Court Act 1989 (Vic)

5 The possibilities of mainstreaming the model

Introduction

> *Mainstream courts are already developing better community connections. . . . The ultimate step in this process would be for a court to operate like a community court or neighbourhood justice centre where the court is not simply reactive but is actively engaging with the community in identifying and resolving justice-related problems.*[1]

A few years after the North Liverpool Community Justice Centre opened, the United Kingdom government decided that instead of replicating the new model, it would be preferable to look at incorporating community justice principles within mainstream courts.[2] This raises a number of important questions. Can Community Justice principles operate within more traditional courtroom models? What changes are necessary to implement more wide-scale justice reform? Might it be that only some Community Justice attributes can be replicated? This chapter looks at the potential benefits of mainstreaming the Community Justice Centre model, exemplars where it has occurred and the barriers and strategies needed to attempt such a task. It concludes that finding ways to build enduring community ties is one of the biggest stumbling blocks for larger scale Community Justice initiatives.

Mainstreaming community justice – the benefits of broadening access

Mainstreaming provides a way to harness the benefits of Community Justice approaches while broadening their access to a wider portion of society,[3] and potentially, doing it more economically. It can still provide interdisciplinary tools to address legal problems while making them available to more judges and to citizens across a wider number of neighbourhoods. In moving away

DOI: 10.4324/9780367823320-5

from the traditional silo-ing of service and justice provision it can present a more efficient means of operation for the criminal justice system. It also means that the benefits of Community Justice, where appropriately evaluated and assessed, could be extended across the justice system to harness the potential for a lowering of crime rates, prison costs and improved order compliance.[4]

Alternative sentencing methods and solution-focused courts, such as drug and mental health courts, have long been looked to for what they might teach the mainstream courts.[5] Accordingly, it is becoming more common to see a variety of more therapeutic processes within courtrooms. One study found that judges who had operated in solution-focused models often favoured transferring alternative approaches to standard court models.[6] Courts are following suit with court liaison officers and interdisciplinary expertise increasingly drawn on in specialist and mainstream court lists.[7] The question is: do more bespoke Community Justice Centre principles have the potential to be applied more broadly across the justice system? This includes not only the attributes that such Centres share with solution-focused innovations (such as seeking to better understand the underlying issues bringing an individual before the court and more therapeutic and procedurally just processes) but also the unique Community Justice focus on a particular locale and the communities within it. Crucially, broadening access to Community Justice principles has the benefit over some specialist solution-focused models of working with a defendant to address the underlying cause/s of criminality through any number of entry points; drug use, homelessness, family violence, unemployment, poverty or mental illness etc.[8]

Examples of mainstreaming

One of the most clear attempts to mainstream the Community Justice Centre model within a wider court system was in Washington DC. Impressed by the success of DC's East of the River Community Court in reducing recidivism, Chief Justice Satterfield determined to rollout a similar approach across Washington DC and without the provision of an increased justice budget.[9] Following a year-long process of stakeholder and community meetings, led by Judge Russell Canan, a 'community court calendar' was instituted in the 'central courthouse' which allocated matters 'by police district', as it was found this would not increase the work from current levels.[10] The reform was very significant. It meant that each judge was allocated the matters from a particular area of DC with a system to change over judges for it to remain sustainable.[11] While the cases were heard centrally the community connection was maintained with community work being completed by defendants in the relevant district and the allocated judge, although 'not embedded in the community', getting to know the district's community and services.[12]

The Hartford Community Court has such a wide operation that it can be seen as a model for mainstreaming. The city's Community Court services 17 localities within Hartford and well as some outer suburbs.[13] It provides needs assessments, community referrals, arranges community meetings and defendants undertaking their excess of 27,000 hours of annual community service locally.[14] It also encourages local involvement with the Court and has a telephone 'hotline' for residents to make suggestions for community service projects.[15]

Other mainstreamed exemplars include Bronx Community Solutions which provides a range of innovative sentencing tools while also looking to collaborate with the Bronx community to contribute to local initiatives as well as getting involved in an 'advisory board'.[16] Community service work is a way that defendants can seek to repair harm to the local community, and suggestions for these emerge from conversations with community members.[17] The Bronx approach centralises the hearing of cases by providing a collaborative model at the Bronx courthouse while also building strong connections with the community. Berman and Fox see this program as an example of 'going to scale' with problem-solving principles when it brings an innovative justice approach to 'nearly two million residents' and 'four dozen judges'.[18]

The Court Integrated Services Program (CISP) runs across the State of Victoria in Australia. It provides defendants, typically those placed on bail, with case management support and referrals both at court and within their local area for services such as drug and alcohol addiction, mental health assistance and housing.[19] While the CISP model is centralised within mainstream Magistrate and County courts it provides a way to link defendants with wrap-around supports through their entry into the court system, usually for a period of three or four months, and with ongoing judicial supervision of their progress.[20] As with Bronx Community Solutions, the program can be accessed by a range of judicial officers and even in cases when a defendant has not pled guilty. The program lacks the local community embeddedness of a typical Community Justice Centre but provides a greater range of supports than traditionally available in metropolitan and regional courthouses.

Barriers to mainstreaming the model

As with many wide-scale justice reforms, cost is a key obstacle to rolling out Community Justice initiatives, whether that be through further pilot projects or a wholesale mainstreamed approach.[21] But it is not just the budgetary impact that becomes a stumbling block. It is also a shortage of trained staff, up-skilled judges, court time and capacity to implement the required community groundwork and planning.[22] For many larger criminal courts the burden of clogged court lists and delayed hearing dates means that finding space for substantive reform can be a real challenge. Mainstreaming requires a concerted remodelling which must be embraced by established courts and their personnel, including amongst the senior judicial ranks. This must then be accompanied by education of the wider justice fraternity including police, prosecutors, defence counsel and allied agencies and departments.[23] Without an awareness of the magnitude of the task, court mainstreaming is unlikely to succeed.[24] As Freiberg notes:

> In an ideal world, it would be pleasing to have, in every court, specialised services staffed with an adequate number of trained staff with the financial resources to meet the full range of offenders' needs. Pending this ideal world, the pragmatic response appears to be to focus these resources in a smaller number of courts which can deal with the more difficult and expensive cases.[25]

It is not just training and resources that need to be prioritised. It is also an associated change in judicial mindset. An acceptance of a reconfigured role for the courts and for judges presents a significant cultural shift and can rub up against engrained notions of the role of judicial officers as independent and impartial decision makers.[26] Community Justice principles also emphasise engagement on an individual and community-level foreign to traditional judging models. Reforms to these established ways of operating need time, planning and adequate consideration of what can be accomplished within that particular jurisdiction and legal framework and within budgetary confines.

Another key barrier to widening the adoption of the Community Justice model is finding a way to retain the 'community' partnership aspect within a centralised or large-scale setting. Along with this is continuing the collaborative aspects, including the co-location of support services, within the Centre. Separating the court from some or all of the services and the local community means that defendant engagement can be more difficult to retain. It also means the court staff need to find innovative ways to retain community rapport, trust and local ownership. For example, Morgan and Brown found that the Neighbourhood Justice Centre compared with the CISP model provided 'better collaboration between service providers and better integration between the court and client services'.[27] This is likely the case both because of the longer periods of sentencing deferral available with the Neighbourhood Justice Centre as well as the proximity of providers. The scaling-up of Community Justice represents a key barrier in terms of how 'to do justice' in an individualised and local way while serving an ever-broader clientele. As Halsey and de Vel-Palumbo found in their research, '[t]he issue of how to maintain model integrity in light of expanding court user and client caseloads is of fundamental import to the ongoing success of community justice centres'.[28]

Mainstreaming can exacerbate concerns as to whether it is appropriate to use the justice system for more widespread service delivery. As explored in Chapter 4, this criticism can be directed at the allocation of resources to justice agencies when it could be that societal and governmental reforms could provide a more efficient means of meeting the needs of citizens without tying it to legal avenues which focus on the individual over wider structural inequalities.

Managing mainstreaming

For mainstreaming to succeed it needs to be in tune with the particular court landscape and the communities served by it. Each jurisdiction has to assess its individual capacity, resourcing and appetite for mainstreaming initiatives and tailor its responses accordingly. For instance, Magistrate Pauline Spencer has noted the benefit in Victoria, Australia, of widespread 'triage and assessment' across a court network to ensure, through '[e]arly intervention' that 'harm to the community' is tapered 'by ensuring people are matched with services at the earliest sign of offending'.[29] Spencer also sees the need for 'mainstream court support available at each court and complex needs interventions available at a regional level' and alongside this a centrally directed 'unit that would oversee continual improvement through evaluation, piloting and dissemination of research and good practice'.[30]

It is also the case that mainstreamed responses need to be attuned to the need for difference both within and between local communities. The new Community Justice Centres being established in Ontario, discussed further in Chapter 6, evidence the difference in need between one area and another and the importance of appreciating that a cookie-cutter approach to rolling out pilots may in fact do more harm than good. For First Nations communities co-creation and leadership of justice initiatives is vital both at the planning and operational stages.

With this wider access through a mainstreamed approach comes the potential, raised in Chapter 4, that citizens may start to experience more from, and accordingly expect more out of, the justice system. While this might not be a problem it can present one if centralised courts implement

Community Justice reforms on a limited or pilot basis or are not able to continue funding them into the future. Admittedly, this can be a difficulty with all justice initiatives and is not an issue solely confined to Community Justice. However, the fundamental renegotiation in the relationship with the community that is observed with Community Justice models means that a heightening of expectations needs to be recognised as part and parcel of the innovation.[31]

Finding ways to develop and retain strong community partnerships is the prime sticking point in mainstreaming the model. While the Washington DC district approach or the Hartford phone hotline show attempts to counter this difficulty, it clearly is one of the most problematic aspects to mainstream. While the judicial officer can visit and get to know the allocated community, it becomes more complex to embed community connection as a consequence of the remoteness of the court's operations. It is also the case that not all local services within the community will be co-located with the central courthouse which means that there may also be gaps in attendance. Some operations of the Centre are also difficult to replicate, especially more local crime prevention or activities interwoven with the community. This presents the possibility of the mainstreamed initiative becoming out of the view of local residents. Magistrate Pauline Spencer has considered many of these issues in the mainstream setting.[32] She recognises that finding time for developing community relationships and linkages requires careful planning amidst a crammed court list, meaning that it becomes 'an additional task undertaken at breakfast, lunch and after court finishes in the afternoon'.[33] She identifies the need for a clear 'community engagement strategy', the use of regular 'court network meetings . . . to break down silos between sectors', 'memorandums of understanding' setting out agreed operating court-agency operations and an online record of relevant support services that can be accessed by all.[34]

What about the dedicated 'one-judge' focus of Community Justice initiatives? Rolling out a model across a city or court network can prevent a judicial officer knowing the residents and community groups in the same way or acquiring the equivalent level of community understanding. It can also mean that you have a number of judges sharing services but severing the close link between one judge and one community as typically seen in a Community Justice Centre. The approach adopted in Washington DC is an example of retaining this singular community connection within a centralised court. This also utilised a rotation approach designed to short-circuit having one judge getting too embedded within a particular community and then potentially causing upheaval when they moved on or retire. While this carries the risk of a weakening in the community–court connection it also could ensure greater longevity of the model.

Conclusion

Mainstreaming Community Justice initiatives can facilitate the potential benefits of Community Justice being available to a wider number of citizens. It is, however, much harder to achieve than more locally focused Community Justice Centre pilots. This is not only through the resources' need for a wider-scale implementation but also the need to train a much large number of judges, stakeholders and agencies about the reform. While providing support services to defendants can bring forward a host of benefits, the challenge becomes finding ways to do so in an integrated way while not necessarily being co-located with the court or the relevant community.

Rolling out Community Justice to mainstream courts is not an impossibility, but it requires considerable planning and community connections to bring about some level of equivalency. It is also likely that those championing mainstream will need to choose what aspects to prioritise in the rollout and what Community Justice Centre dimensions will not be able to be as easily reproduced. The focus will need to be on careful planning, extensive training and a deep understanding of the particular jurisdiction. Ultimately, it is the degree of community embeddedness that is likely to be the hardest aspect to fully replicate in the mainstream.

Notes

1 Michael King, 'What Can Mainstream Courts Learn from Problem-Solving Courts' (2007) 32(2) *Alternative Law Journal* 91, 94.
2 UK Ministry of Justice, 'Green Paper – Engaging Communities in Criminal Justice', April 2009, www.gov.uk/government/uploads/system/uploads/attachment_data/file/228540/7583.pdf
3 Lorana Bartels, 'Challenges in Mainstreaming Specialty Courts' (2009) October *Trends & Issues in Crime and Criminal Justice* 1, 2.
4 Ibid. 3.
5 See, e.g. Donald J. Farole et al., 'Applying Problem-Solving Principles in Mainstream Courts: Lessons for State Courts' (2005) 26(1) *Justice System Journal* 57. King, 'What Can Mainstream Courts Learn from Problem-Solving Courts', above n 1, 91; Bartels, 'Challenges in Mainstreaming Specialty Courts', above n 3; Pauline Spencer, 'From Alternative to the New Normal: Therapeutic Jurisprudence in the Mainstream' (2014) 39(4) *Alternative Law Journal* 222; Pauline Spencer, 'To Dream the Impossible Dream? Therapeutic Jurisprudence in Mainstream Courts' (2012) 22 *Journal of Judicial Administration* 85.
6 Greg Berman and John Feinblatt, *Good Courts – The Case for Problem-Solving Justice* (New York Press, 2005) 196.
7 See, e.g. King, 'What Can Mainstream Courts Learn from Problem-Solving Courts', above n 1, 93.
8 Bartels, 'Challenges in Mainstreaming Specialty Courts', above n 3, 2.
9 Sarah Schweig, *Beyond a Single Neighborhood* (Center for Court Innovation, 2014) 2. See also Julius Lang, *What Is a Community Court? How the*

Model Is Being Adapted Across the United States (Bureau of Justice Assistance, 2011) 5, www.courtinnovation.org/publications/what-community-court-how-model-being-adapted-across-united-states

10 Schweig, *Beyond a Single Neighborhood*, above n 9, 2–3.
11 Ibid. 3.
12 Ibid. 3–4.
13 Lang, *What Is a Community Court?* above n 9, 10.
14 Center for Court Innovation, 'Hartford Community Court', www.courtinnovation.org/sites/default/files/documents/HartfordBrochure.pdf
15 Lang, *What Is a Community Court?* above n 9, 7.
16 Ibid. 13.
17 Ibid.
18 Greg Berman and Aubrey Fox, 'The Future of Problem-Solving Justice: An International Perspective' (2010) 10 *University of Maryland Law & Justice Race, Religion, Gender & Class* 1, 11–12.
19 Magistrates' Court of Victoria, 'Bail Support (CISP)', https://mcv.vic.gov.au/find-support/bail-support-cisp; County Court Victoria, 'Court Integrated Services Program', www.countycourt.vic.gov.au/going-court/criminal-division/court-integrated-services-program
20 See also Bartels, 'Challenges in Mainstreaming Specialty Courts', above n 3, 2–3.
21 Farole et al., 'Applying Problem-Solving Principles in Mainstream Courts', above n 5, 66.
22 Ibid. 67–8. King, 'What Can Mainstream Courts Learn from Problem-Solving Courts', above n 1, 94.
23 See, e.g. Spencer, 'From Alternative to the New Normal', above n 5, 224.
24 Berman and Fox, 'The Future of Problem-Solving Justice', above n 18, 20.
25 Arie Freiberg, 'Problem-Oriented Courts: Innovative Solutions to Intractable Problems?' (2011) 11 *Journal of Judicial Administration* 8, 22.
26 See further, Bartels, 'Challenges in Mainstreaming Specialty Courts', above n 3, 4; Berman and Feinblatt, *Good Courts*, above n 6, 196.
27 Anthony Morgan and Rick Brown, 'Estimating the Costs Associated with Community Justice' (2015) 507 *Trends & Issues in Crime and Criminal Justice* 10, www.aic.gov.au/publications/tandi/tandi507
28 Mark Halsey and Melissa de Vel-Palumbo, 'Courts as Empathic Spaces: Reflections on the Neighbourhood Justice Centre' (2018) 27(2) *Griffith Law Review* 182, 198.
29 Spencer, 'From Alternative to the New Normal', above n 5, 225.
30 Ibid.
31 Sarah Murray, 'Keeping It in the Neighbourhood? Neighbourhood Courts in the Australian Context' (2009) 35(1) *Monash University Law Review* 74, 124.
32 Spencer, 'To Dream the Impossible Dream?', above n 5, 93.
33 Ibid.
34 Ibid. 93–4.

Bibliography

Bartels, Lorana. 'Challenges in Mainstreaming Specialty Courts' (2009) October *Trends & Issues in Crime and Criminal Justice* 1.

Berman, Greg and John Feinblatt. *Good Courts – The Case for Problem-Solving Justice* (New York Press, 2005).

Berman, Greg and Aubrey Fox. 'The Future of Problem-Solving Justice: An International Perspective' (2010) 10 *University of Maryland Law Journal of Race, Religion, Gender and Class* 1.

Center for Court Innovation. 'Hartford Community Court', www.courtinnovation. org/sites/default/files/documents/HartfordBrochure.pdf

County Court Victoria. 'Court Integrated Services Program', www.countycourt.vic. gov.au/going-court/criminal-division/court-integrated-services-program

Farole, Donald J. et al. 'Applying Problem-Solving Principles in Mainstream Courts: Lessons for State Courts' (2005) 26(1) *Justice System Journal* 57.

Freiberg, Arie. 'Problem-Oriented Courts: Innovative Solutions to Intractable Problems?' (2011) 11 *Journal of Judicial Administration* 8.

Halsey, Mark and Melissa de Vel-Palumbo. 'Courts as Empathic Spaces: Reflections on the Neighbourhood Justice Centre' (2018) 27(2) *Griffith Law Review* 182.

King, Michael. 'What Can Mainstream Courts Learn from Problem-Solving Courts' (2007) 32(2) *Alternative Law Journal* 91.

Lang, Julius. *What Is a Community Court? How the Model Is Being Adapted Across the United States* (Bureau of Justice Assistance, 2011), 5, www.courtinnovation. org/publications/what-community-court-how-model-being-adapted-across-united-states

Magistrates' Court of Victoria. 'Bail Support (CISP)', https://mcv.vic.gov.au/ find-support/bail-support-cisp

Morgan, Anthony and Rick Brown. 'Estimating the Costs Associated with Community Justice' (2015) 507 *Trends & Issues in Crime and Criminal Justice* 10, www. aic.gov.au/publications/tandi/tandi507

Murray, Sarah. 'Keeping It in the Neighbourhood? Neighbourhood Courts in the Australian Context' (2009) 35(1) *Monash University Law Review* 74.

Schweig, Sarah. *Beyond a Single Neighborhood* (Center for Court Innovation, 2014).

Spencer, Pauline. 'From Alternative to the New Normal: Therapeutic Jurisprudence in the Mainstream' (2014) 39(4) *Alternative Law Journal* 222.

Spencer, Pauline. 'To Dream the Impossible Dream? Therapeutic Jurisprudence in Mainstream Courts' (2012) 22 *Journal of Judicial Administration* 85.

UK Ministry of Justice. 'Green Paper – Engaging Communities in Criminal Justice', April 2009, www.gov.uk/government/uploads/system/uploads/attachment_data/ file/228540/7583.pdf

6 Conclusion
The future of community justice: prospects and challenges

Introduction

Community Justice Centres are a growing area of interest within criminal justice. Ontario is embarking on a radical shake-up of its court-system with planning for four new Community Justice Centres underway: the Kenora Bi-Community Justice Centre, the London Justice Centre and Centres in Toronto–Downtown East and Toronto–Northwest.[1] While its formal opening was delayed by COVID-19, the Inverness Justice Centre in Scotland opened its doors in March 2020, bringing together a court alongside a host of linked services.[2] This concluding chapter appraises the Community Justice landscape and delineates the outlook for this collaborative and locally embedded justice model.

Foretelling the future for community justice

One of the key questions for the Community Justice model is: what will be its lasting influence on the justice system? Certainly, like with more solution-focused court models, changing political dynamics can impact on the rise or fall of innovative reforms like Community Justice Centres. Fundamentally, the future of Community Justice rests in demonstrating that ' "community" and "justice" ' while 'not always in perfect harmony . . . are not in fact oppositional forces'.[3] And for individual Community Justice Centres there is a need to continually reinvent the community relationship and connection and ensure that the Centre remains attuned to local need and local transformation.

Heterogeneity

As a consequence of the diversity between and within neighbourhoods, Community Justice Centres are far from homogenous.[4] This is likely to

DOI: 10.4324/9780367823320-6

become more pronounced if the model continues to attract wider interest. For instance, Brownsville Community Justice Center, was one of the first Centres to be established without a co-located courthouse. Similarly the Spokane Municipal Community Court housed in a public library on an assigned day each week, demonstrates the flexibility of the model and how it can adopt more ambulatory and economical formats.[5] There is also interest in a variety of multi-door models which co-locate a range of services[6] and which draw on aspects of community justice while not necessarily operating alongside a court.

Newman has noted the need to identify what is and what is not 'Community Justice' in action: '[w]e have to be careful to not let it get too broad a concept or to sweep too much within it, because at some point it will be such an umbrella that it won't mean anything'.[7] This is particularly pertinent as the model matures and different exemplars are grafted. However, it is also the case that Community Justice Centres have consistently drawn on elements of other less-adversarial models just as other models draw on elements of Community Justice. The core attributes typically associated with a Community Justice Centre – a Centre that is community-designed and connected to deliver local place-based justice solutions – seem the most evident parallel across varied exemplars, whether or not the Community Justice appellation remains habitually applied.

Co-design and co-creation

Community co-design and co-creation is going to be pivotal to the future of the Community Justice model when it is centred on the notion that 'citizens and neighbourhood groups' have 'an active voice in doing justice'.[8] Amongst diverse communities this is all the more important but needs to be carefully planned. It also needs to be done slowly to mobilise a strong support base when '[f]ast tracking the creation of a community court to meet the schedules or demands of elected officials, funders or other interested parties invariably creates as many problems as it solves'.[9]

How do you ensure that some groups or subgroups are not marginalised in the planning processes? This is particularly important in relation to groups that have been historically silenced such as First Nations communities.[10] For instance the new Kenora Centre is adopting a 'participatory design process' working with local community leaders.[11] What innovative means can be adopted to promote involvement from diverse interest groups within a neighbourhood? How is community involvement built in at all stages of a pilot – initial planning, consultation, implementation and evaluation – and how is this maintained as its operation becomes more routine? Finding ways to answer this and ensure that a Centre retains legitimacy and community buy-in is fundamental. As Berman articulated, '[t]here is no magic recipe for creating a community court. . . . [J]urisdictions will inevitably have to improvise to respond to unique conditions on the ground'.[12]

The important of co-creation and co-design extends to the operation of Community Justice Centres as well, not only in terms of retaining authentic community-controlled processes and active citizen engagement but also in terms of the court itself. This even extends to the relationship of the bench and the defendant. It shouldn't be thought that a defendant appearing before a community court is transformed by that appearance alone. As King generally explains, 'the source of change is within the participants; their attitude to change and to the process is the prime determinant of the success of any problem-solving court'.[13]

Interdisciplinarity

Therapeutic jurisprudence, procedural justice and restorative justice, as core principles at the heart of community justice, highlight the fundamental potential of interdisciplinarity for the criminal justice system. Community Justice Centres and solution-focused models recognise that the law is not going to always solve a problem, and if it does, it may not prevent that problem re-emerging. One of the key innovations of Community Justice is positioning a range of experts alongside a court so that the community can access those services easily and in a one-stop model. In providing treatment and support in proximity to a court appearance, courts are able to capitalise on the 'legal moment' and the authority of the court to motivate a defendant to change. For many Centres the services are available to all community members without the need to have a matter before the court. With the Brownsville Community Justice Center this service model has developed to serve justice ends even in the absence of a courthouse.

It is important to also see the limits of interdisciplinarity. While this wrap-around service model holds much potential for the justice system more broadly, it is inevitable that some defendants will still slip through the cracks. For many individuals personal change is a very complex process involving a range of intersecting life circumstances, and the model simply makes change more possible than it might otherwise be. Additionally, for some defendants it may be that access to the co-located services is not appropriate or even necessary.

Community Justice Centres raise ongoing questions about the appropriate role that courts should play and whether services are best delivered outside of the justice system. While requiring ongoing appraisal and research, such Centres provide one way to change the one-track legal response to be more holistic while not precluding other service delivery avenues. The net impact on community resources is, however, an important issue to examine to ensure that services are not being removed only to the 'back end'.[14] Their availability and cross-referability also present an innovative way of tackling the growing silo-ing of services and the tendency for constant on-referrals. As Kylie Smith, the Koori Justice Worker at the Neighbourhood Justice Centre explained, '[c]reating a connection between community, outside services and the justice system provides a softer edge'.[15]

For judicial officers, lawyers and the justice system, Community Justice Centres require a different way of doing law. It requires careful calibration to ensure that justice is still administered independently and impartially. Therapeutic jurisprudence has long recognised that there are occasions where the law must trump other considerations to ensure that justice is fairly delivered.[16] However, it is also about looking for opportunities to practise law in a way that might leave a positive imprint on individuals, families and communities.

Evaluating and re-evaluating evaluations

The success of Community Justice prototypes is contingent on stemming the 'damage that crime can do to both individuals and communities'.[17] This requires properly planned and operated Centres that are in tune with community need and jurisdictional demands. It also requires the employment of evaluative tools that assess the holistic impact of Centres. Innovative data collection methods, both qualitative and quantitative, are vital to track community well-being, and stories of success as well as more standard indicators such as recidivism, the rate of case closure and order compliance. As Berman has recognised 'by changing the questions asked of the justice system, it is often possible to change the behavior of those who work within the system'.[18]

As Centres become entrenched they need to continually find ways to monitor their goals and compliance with them. For many Centres this will require strong community partnerships that engage with and listen to local residents, schools, police and businesses to avoid operational complacency and prioritise innovation. In terms of accountability it is also important that staff don't lift expectations beyond what can realistically be achieved by a Centre. Inflating the hopes of locals can result in a decline in a Centre's legitimacy and acceptance and can threaten to undo much work that has been done in developing community rapport and establishing vital networks.

Evaluation and appropriate benchmarking remains a priority not only to respond to requests from justice agencies and funders but also to develop and retain public confidence in a Centre and community perceptions of safety. As Karafin notes:

> meaningfully monitoring the impact of community courts on communities, offenders, victims and the criminal justice system as a whole should be considered a top priority as the model is replicated and introduced to new contexts.[19]

The record of Centres so far is that if carefully operationalised and appraised, they can have notable justice outcomes, from reduced recidivism and prison time to a reduction in local crime and an increase in community perceptions of safety, well-being and the experience in coming to court.[20]

Rolling out?

The perennial question – if a Centre proves successful – is whether its benefits can be extended through further Centres or whether some of the Centre's tactics can be tapped into by traditional courts through wider mainstreaming? This issue was discussed in much detail in Chapter 5.

If further Centres are being explored, it is vital that the Centres are not designed as cookie-cutter versions of the primary Centre. Each Centre, such as the many examples that have emerged in New York, need to have bespoke planning and consultation to consider what design aspects can be drawn upon and what needs to be reconsidered for a particular neighbourhood. For example, a different community may require quite a different jurisdiction for the court and a range of unique support services. In Ontario, the four new centres that are planned have very different central focuses – bi-cultural approach, 'community health', 'community violence' and youth.[21]

It may well be that a Community Justice solution is not appropriate at a particular point in time, and planners need to be willing to accept that and listen to the priorities that the community articulates in its place. Restricted budgets or resources may also taper what is possible even if a new pilot is to be explored.

Mainstreaming provides a way to broaden the number of cases resolved through Community Justice avenues. Such a move is, however, complex. If aspects of the Community Justice model are to be funded within a centralised courthouse, what aspects are to be prioritised? For example, how will the connection with community be established and maintained? Will a crime prevention team be possible within a centralised model? How is the training and stakeholder education to be managed amidst overcrowded court case lists? How will service provision be managed, and will this compromise the co-location of services with the court? Mainstreaming requires a pragmatic assessment of what is feasible and requires readiness, knowledge and resources to be achievable.

Conclusion

Community Justice Centres cannot be seen as a panacea for all criminal justice woes. They require planning, staff training, assessment and ongoing innovation to remain in tune with changing community needs and expectations. If prudently managed, however, they can provide a way to reconfigure the relationship between the justice system and the community. By partnering with residents, community stakeholders and agencies, Community Justice Centres present a means of expanding solutions beyond the legal frame. They also can contribute to a heightening court legitimacy[22] and a new understanding of the difference that they can make to a community. As Rottman foresaw over 20 years ago:

> Ultimately, the challenge of creating community-focused courts may lie with communities themselves. The low level of public knowledge about courts is a formidable obstacle to collaboration between courts and communities. For this obstacle to be overcome, organized community interests need to view the courts as a resource and as a vehicle for change. In other words, if there are to be community-focused courts, there must be court-focused communities.[23]

Notes

1 Ministry of the Attorney-General, 'Justice Centres', 2 October 2020, www.attorneygeneral.jus.gov.on.ca/english/justice-centres/; Ministry of the Attorney-General, 'Community Justice Centres', 2018, https://hsjcc.on.ca/wp-content/uploads/NY-HSJCC-Community-Justice-Centres.pdf
2 Scottish Courts and Tribunals, 'Inverness Justice Centre', 2020, www.lawreform.ie/news/law-reform-commission-publishes-report-on-accessibility-of-legislation-in-the-digital-age.884.html
3 Greg Berman and Aubrey Fox, 'From the Benches and Trenches- Justice in Red Hook' (2005) 26(1) *Justice System Journal* 77, 88.
4 David B. Rottman, 'Community Courts: Prospects and Limits' (1996) 231 *National Institute of Justice Journal* 46, 50.
5 The initiative has also spread to public libraries in Nevada and Oregon: Caitlin Flood and Emily LaGratta, *Spokane's Library Community Court Model* (Center for Court Innovation, 2020) 7.
6 In Australia see, e.g. First Step, 'First Step', www.firststep.org.au/, Ruah Community Services, 'Ruah Community Services', www.ruah.org.au/

7 Quoted in Greg Berman and Aubrey Fox, 'From the Margins to the Mainstream: Community Justice at the Crossroads' (2001) 22(2) *Justice System Journal* 189, 191.

8 Greg Berman, *Principles of Community Justice – A Guide for Community Court Planners* (Center for Court Innovation, 2010) 7, www.courtinnovation.org/ sites/default/files/Communitycourtprinciples.pdf

9 Ibid. 12.

10 See, e.g. Aleksandra Miller, 'Neighbourhood Justice Centres and Indigenous Empowerment' (2017) 20 *Australian Indigenous Law Review* 123, 143–4.

11 Ministry of the Attorney-General, 'Justice Centres – Presentation for the Toronto Aboriginal Affairs Advisory Committee', 11 February 2020, 8, www.toronto.ca/ legdocs/mmis/2020/aa/bgrd/backgroundfile-145736.pdf

12 Berman, *Principles of Community Justice*, above n 8, 15.

13 Michael King, 'What Can Mainstream Courts Learn from Problem-Solving Courts' (2007) 32(2) *Alternative Law Journal* 91.

14 Corey Shdaimah, 'Taking a Stand in a Not-So-Perfect World: What's a Critical Supporter of Problem-Solving Courts to Do?' (2010) 10(1) *University of Maryland Law Journal of Race, Religion, Gender and Class* 89, 101.

15 Kylie Smith, 'Reflections on the Design, Country and Community Justice at the Neighbourhood Justice Centre' (2018) 27(2) *Griffith Law Review* 202, 205.

16 See chapter 1.

17 John Feinblatt and Greg Berman, 'Community Courts: A Brief Primer' (2001) January *United States Attorney's Bulletin* 33, 37.

18 Berman, *Principles of Community Justice*, above n 8, 10.

19 Diana L. Karafin, 'Community Courts Across the Globe: A Survey of Goals, Performance Measures and Operations', 2008, 25, www.courtinnovation.org/ sites/default/files/community_court_world.pdf

20 See, e.g. Avram Bornstein et al., 'Tell It to the Judge: Procedural Justice and the Community Court in Brooklyn' (2016) 39(2) *Political and Legal Anthropological Review* 206.

21 Ministry of the Attorney-General, 'Justice Centres – Presentation for the Toronto Aboriginal Affairs Advisory Committee', above n 11, 7–8.

22 Berman and Fox, 'From the Margins to the Mainstream', above n 6, 195 (Lane); 206 (Feinblatt). See also Christine Zozula, 'Courting the Community: Organizational Flexibility and Community Courts' (2018) 18(2) *Criminology & Criminal Justice* 226.

23 Rottman, 'Community Courts: Prospects and Limits', above n 4, 51.

Bibliography

Berman, Greg. *Principles of Community Justice – A Guide for Community Court Planners* (Center for Court Innovation, 2010), www.courtinnovation.org/sites/ default/files/Communitycourtprinciples.pdf

Berman, Greg and Aubrey Fox. 'From the Benches and Trenches- Justice in Red Hook' (2005) 26(1) *The Justice System Journal* 77.

Berman, Greg and Aubrey Fox. 'From the Margins to the Mainstream: Community Justice at the Crossroads" (2001) 22(2) *Justice System Journal* 189.

Bornstein, Avram et al. 'Tell It to the Judge: Procedural Justice and the Community Court in Brooklyn' (2016) 39(2) *Political and Legal Anthropological Review* 206.

Feinblatt, John and Greg Berman. 'Community Courts: A Brief Primer' (2001) January *United States Attorney's Bulletin* 33.

First Step. 'First Step', www.firststep.org.au/

Flood, Caitlin and Emily LaGratta. *Spokane's Library Community Court Model* (Center for Court Innovation, 2020).

Karafin, Diana L. 'Community Courts Across the Globe: A Survey of Goals, Performance Measures and Operations', 2008, www.courtinnovation.org/sites/default/files/community_court_world.pdf

King, Michael. 'What Can Mainstream Courts Learn from Problem-Solving Courts' (2007) 32(2) *Alternative Law Journal* 91.

Miller, Aleksandra. 'Neighbourhood Justice Centres and Indigenous Empowerment' (2017) 20 *Australian Indigenous Law Review* 123.

Ministry of the Attorney-General. 'Community Justice Centres', 2018, https://hsjcc.on.ca/wp-content/uploads/NY-HSJCC-Community-Justice-Centres.pdf

Ministry of the Attorney-General. 'Justice Centres', 2 October 2020, www.attorneygeneral.jus.gov.on.ca/english/justice-centres/

Ministry of the Attorney-General. 'Justice Centres – Presentation for the Toronto Aboriginal Affairs Advisory Committee', 11 February 2020, www.toronto.ca/legdocs/mmis/2020/aa/bgrd/backgroundfile-145736.pdf

Rottman, David B. 'Community Courts: Prospects and Limits' (1996) 231 *National Institute of Justice Journal* 46.

Ruah Community Services. 'Ruah Community Services', www.ruah.org.au/

Scottish Courts and Tribunals. 'Inverness Justice Centre', 2020, www.lawreform.ie/news/law-reform-commission-publishes-report-on-accessibility-of-legislation-in-the-digital-age.884.html

Shdaimah, Corey. 'Taking a Stand in a Not-So-Perfect World: What's a Critical Supporter of Problem-Solving Courts to Do?' (2010) 10(1) *University of Maryland Law Journal of Race, Religion, Gender and Class* 89.

Smith, Kylie. 'Reflections on the Design, Country and Community Justice at the Neighbourhood Justice Centre' (2018) 27(2) *Griffith Law Review* 202.

Zozula, Christine. 'Courting the Community: Organizational Flexibility and Community Courts' (2018) 18(2) *Criminology & Criminal Justice* 226.

Index